MICHIGAN
Off the Beaten Path

"A rare publication that provides a mixture of those 'don't miss' attractions and many that really are off the beaten path and usually missed by the visitor."
> —**Chris Dancisak**, executive manager, Upper Peninsula and Recreation Association

"**Michigan: Off the Beaten Path** is an essential traveling companion for anyone who enjoys the gentle rhythms of small towns, natural wonders, and the sort of roadside attractions that have been passed by freeways."
> —**Changing Homes** magazine

"Hit the country roads and explore the hidden gems ... that Du-Fresne has discovered."
> —The **Saginaw News**

"... Lives up to its subtitle, 'A Guide to Unique Places' ... a nicely written, easy-to-use guide ... will come in handy whether you're on a full-scale vacation in Wolverine land or just planning a nice, long Sunday drive."
> —The **Flint (MI) Journal**

MICHIGAN
Off the Beaten Path

by **Jim DuFresne**

A Voyager Book

Chester, Connecticut

Reprinted Summer 1988

Library of Congress Cataloging-in-Publication Data

DuFresne, Jim.
    Michigan: off the beaten path.

    (A Voyager book)
    Includes index.
    1. Michigan — Description and travel —
Guide-books. I. Title.
F564.3.D84   1988   917.74'0443   87-37362
ISBN 0-87106-791-9 (pbk.)

Manufactured in the United States of America
First Edition/Third Printing

Acknowledgments

She was sitting alongside a bumpy county road, sitting on a wooden cart she had used to haul bushels of peaches down from the barn. She was sitting there enjoying the early morning sun, the fragrance of fruit ripening in the surrounding orchards, waving to people going by that she knew.

She wasn't hawking. She was much too old for that. But a simple hand-painted sign leaning against the cart revealed her intentions: "Peaches 4 Sale."

I was in Berrien County, trying to find my way to Tabor Hill Vineyards, when I saw her and had to stop. We chatted, we bargained, and finally we decided that I could use a quarter bushel of Red Haven peaches for $2.

The peaches in their basket sat next to me on the front seat of my truck and I picked up one off the top and took a bite. There was an explosion of juice.

This was one ripe Red Haven peach. The juice sprayed over my cheeks, ran down the front of my shirt, dripped onto the steering wheel, dribbled onto my pants.

But I didn't mind. On that early morning in the countryside, nothing could have tasted sweeter. I made my way to the vineyard driving 10 miles an hour and leaning my head out the window for every bite of this Michigan treat.

Just another pleasant memory from a summer that was filled with them. I grew up in this state and have spent most of my days here. But I came home in the summer of 1987 when I took to the country roads, the "blue highways" as one author calls them, and spent four months searching Michigan.

Some 8,000 miles later I was done and so was this book. It was an incredible adventure in a state so dear to me. And it couldn't have been possible without the help of many.

I stayed with friends all over the state who provided not only a soft bed and a hot meal at night but an insight into their region of Michigan. There were Carl Hubinger and his family in Au Train of the Upper Peninsula, Tom and Andree Almer in Lansing, Mark Romanack in Saginaw, Eleanor DeBaene in Harbor Springs, Bob and Lissa Lutz in St. Joseph, Allan Lengal in East Lansing, my parents in Elk Rapids.

Right from the beginning I was encouraged by my wife, Peggy, an enthusiastic traveler in her own right and someone who knows what makes a good guidebook. Neither one of us could have survived the summer without the assistance of Amy Jeschawitz, who managed our affairs at home, not to mention our two children.

Most of all I am indebted to every employee of every tourist bureau, chamber of commerce, and visitor's center; to every traveler at every rest area, roadside park, and gas station; to everybody who told me of another place to see and visit. These are the people who helped me discover the wonders of Michigan.

Illustrations by Steve Baldwin
Cover illustration of Port Sanilac Lighthouse by Pamela Hopson
Typography by TRG

To that wonderfully warm and huggable person I call Mom.

Michigan

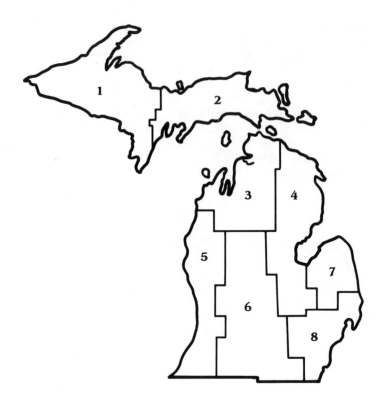

Contents

Introduction

Look at a map of the United States, spin a globe of the world, and the most prominent state is Michigan. It always stands out regardless of the size of the map or how obscured the detail.

Michigan is set off from the rest of the country by water. Four of the five Great Lakes surround it and have turned most of its borders into 3,200 miles of lake shore where you sit in the sand and look out on the watery horizon of the world's largest freshwater seas.

Michigan is inundated by water. It's not only outlined by blue, but its history was shaped by the Great Lakes and today travelers search the state over for a bit of their own sand and surf. In Michigan, there is no short supply. Stand anywhere in the state and you are no more than 85 miles from the Great Lakes and only 6 miles from one of the 11,000 sparkling inland lakes or 36,000 miles of streams and rivers. Come winter, Michigan's water turns fluffy and white and gently lands all around, much to the delight of skiers.

Michigan is water, yet beaches and boating, swimming and sunbathing are only part of the attractions the state has to offer. To the adventurous traveler, to those who love to swing off the interstate highways onto the country roads that wander between the woods and the lakes, there are quaint villages to discover and shipwrecks to explore, art fairs and mushroom festivals to enjoy, wine-tasting tours to savor, a stretch of quiet trail to soothe the urban soul.

All you need is time, a good map of Michigan, and this book. The map can be obtained from the Michigan Travel Bureau by writing (P.O. Box 30226, Lansing, MI 48909) or by calling a toll-free number (800-543-2937). The map will lead you away from the six-lane highways to the scenic country roads and then back again when you are ready to return home.

Michigan: Off the Beaten Path points out those half-hidden gems that travelers rejoice in discovering, from a lighthouse that has become a country inn to party fishing boats that allow novice anglers to stalk and catch the Great Lakes' tastiest offering, the yellow perch. Because addresses, phone numbers, and hours of operation can change from summer to summer, in the appendix there is a list of regional tourist associations that can provide the most up-to-date information.

The same holds true for prices. Inflation, with its annual increases in everything from room rates and entree prices to entry fees into parks and museums, will quickly outdate anything listed. Therefore only the prices for substantial items (rooms, meals, and major attractions) have been provided in this book to help readers judge whether a restaurant or hotel is affordable.

But most of all, more than this book and a map, you need time. Don't shortchange Michigan. Don't try to cover half the state in a weekend holiday. You will only be disappointed at the end of your trip. You could spend a summer exploring Michigan and never leave the shoreline. I have spent a lifetime here, yet my never-ending list of places to go and adventures to undertake only grows longer with each journey in the Great Lakes State.

Off the Beaten Path in Southeast Michigan

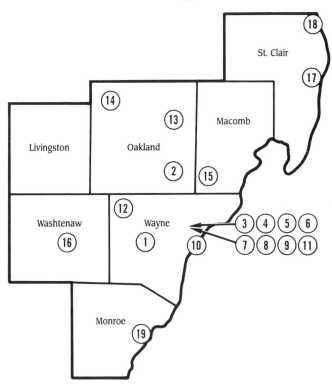

St. Clair

Macomb

Oakland

Livingston

Washtenaw

Wayne

Monroe

1. Fairlane Mansion in Dearborn
2. Meadow Brook Hall in Rochester
3. Riverfront Festivals at Hart Plaza
4. Eastern Market/
   R. Hirt Jr., Import Co.
5. Tiger Stadium
6. Lafayette Coney Island
7. Brother's Bar-B-Q
8. People Mover
9. Chene Park
10. SS *Columbia* and SS *Ste. Claire*
    historic steamships
11. Detroit Institute of Arts
12. Maybury State Park
13. Bald Mountain Recreation Area
14. Holly/Battle Alley/Holly Hotel
15. Yates Cider Mill
16. Ann Arbor/Ann Arbor Hands-On
    Museum/Kerrytown Shops
17. Riverwalk Park in St. Clair
18. Port Huron/Boat Night/The
    Victorian Inn/Port Huron
    Museum of Art And History
19. The Monroe County Historical
    Museum

Southeast Michigan

Southeast Michigan, a region of seven counties, revolves around metropolitan Detroit, which sprawls into three of them. And Detroit revolves around automobiles. It's as simple as that.

Known best throughout the country as Motor City, Detroit carries several other titles, including Motown after the recording company that produced such famous singers as Diana Ross and Stevie Wonder before it fled to Los Angeles from its studio on Woodward Avenue. Detroit also has the distinction of being the only city in the United States that lies *north* of Canada. Visitors are surprised when they have to drive south on the Ambassador Bridge to reach Windsor, Ontario.

Detroit and its neighboring suburbs wear many faces; some are good, some are unjustly earned, but the least-recognized one is that of a destination for travelers. Detroit is the sixth-largest city in the country, yet despite its size many tourists consider it very much "off the beaten path." Depart from the city and the rest of Southeast Michigan changes quickly, from the urban sprawl to the rolling hills and lakes of northern Oakland County, the blue water of St. Clair and Port Huron, and the culture and carefree college ways of Ann Arbor, the home of the University of Michigan.

Wayne County

Until the 1870s, Detroit was a commercial center for farmers, but at the end of that century the first automobiles appeared as Ransom E. Olds and Henry Ford began tinkering with "horseless carriages." By 1903, Ford had organized the Ford Motor Company, and when he pioneered the assembly-line method of building cars and introduced the Model T, the vehicle for the common man, Detroit's place as the automobile capital of the world was determined.

Cars are a way of life in Detroit. Michigan boasts of having the first mile of concrete rural highway (1909), the first traffic light (1915), and the first urban freeway free of those annoying stoplights (1942). The best-known place to view this history of cars and its immense effect on the American way of life is Greenfield

Village and Henry Ford Museum (313-271-1620), a 260-acre complex with one hundred historic buildings in Dearborn that has become the nation's largest indoor and outdoor museum.

But for a more intimate view of the auto barons themselves, visit one of the many mansions that auto money built and historical societies have since preserved. **Fairlane,** the Henry Ford estate, is a fifty-six–room mansion located nearby on the University of Michigan–Dearborn Campus. Built in 1915 at what was then an astronomical $1.8 million, the home is an extension of Ford's ingenuity wrapped up in his love for functionalism. It often hosted such dignitaries as Thomas Edison, President Herbert Hoover, and Charles Lindbergh. Tours begin underground among the massive turbines and generators that were designed by Ford and his friend Edison in the six-level powerhouse that made the estate self-sufficient in power, heat, light, even ice.

From the outside the house looks modest compared to other historic mansions. But inside you'll find such luxuries as a central vacuum cleaner, a sixty-five–extension phone system, a one-lane bowling alley, and a pool which has been covered and turned into a delightful restaurant that serves lunch. Guided tours lead you through the house and underground tunnels, show you where Edison used to sleep, and tell of April 7, 1947, when the Rouge River flooded and knocked out the powerhouse. That night, without heat, light, or phone service, Ford suffered a cerebral hemorrhage and died by candlelight.

To reach U of M—Dearborn head west of Southfield Expressway on Michigan Avenue and then north on Greenfield Road, where signs point the way to the small campus. Guided tours of the national historic landmark are offered year-round on Sunday from 1 to 4 P.M. From May 1 through Sept. 30 Fairlane (313-593-5590) is also open Monday through Saturday from 10 A.M. to 4 P.M. There is an admission fee.

To most people Detroit is Motor City, but to music lovers it will always be Motown, the birthplace of the famous record company that Berry Gordy, Jr. founded in 1960. Gordy started out with $800 and a small recording studio that was built in the back of his Grand Boulevard home. From Studio A emerged the distinct "Motown Sound" and such performers as Marvin Gaye, the Miracles, Gladys Knight and the Pips, the Supremes, The Jackson 5 and a very talented blind singer named Steveland Morris Hardaway, known now as Stevie Wonder. Eventually the famous "Hitsville,

3

U.S.A." sign was hung on the front of the home and Motown expanded into seven additional houses along the street before setting up in its Woodward office.

But the company continued recording in Studio A until 1972 when it moved its operation to Los Angeles. What remains today at Hitsville U.S.A. is **Motown Museum**, a state historic site. The museum is two adjoining houses filled with gold record awards, old album covers, publicity photos and even some old Temptation costumes that are viewed to the beat of Motown hits played continuously in every room. But for most visitors the intriguing part is Studio A and its control booth, looking as it did 25 years ago when Motown was a struggling recording company.

Motown Museum (313-875-2264) is located at 2648 West Grand Boulevard two blocks west of the exit off of the Lodge Freeway. The museum is open Monday through Friday from 10 a.m. to 5 p.m. and Sunday 2 p.m. to 5 p.m. There is a small admission fee.

Detroit has its mansions and its auto barons, but it is known primarily as a blue-collar town, an assembly-line haven that has made it as ethnically diverse as any city in the country. Detroiters love their heritage, their ethnic foods, their music, and the traditions of an old way of life somewhere else. This is seen in the **Riverfront Festivals** held each weekend of the summer at Hart Plaza at the foot of Woodward Avenue downtown. Each one is devoted to a different nationality, and from 11:30 A.M. Friday until 10 P.M. Sunday the Detroit River plaza is filled with music, dancing, and entertainment that is free and with the aroma of specialty dishes and other tempting morsels that are inexpensive. The best ones—the Polish Festival, German Festival, and Afro-American Festival—tend to reflect the larger segments of the city's population. For current themes and dates, call the Ethnic Festival Hotline (313-224-1184).

This ethnic pride and the love of traditional foods can also be seen at the **Eastern Market**, a farmer's market that is said to be the largest of its kind in the country. Two halls, one open-air, one enclosed, and both decorated with huge murals on the outside, are the heart of the market. On Tuesdays and Saturdays they overflow with shoppers, farmers, and vendors bartering for the freshest fruit, vegetables, flowers, meats, and cheeses to be found in the city. Everything from the farm is on sale here, from homemade bratwurst to live rabbits, and the market makes for an enjoyable stroll even if you don't intend to buy anything.

**R. Hirt Jr., Co. in Detroit's
Eastern Market**

Ringing the market are butcher shops, fish markets, and stores specializing in spices, nuts, or foods imported from around the world. The oldest shop is **R. Hirt Jr. Importer**, in a three-story red brick building that overlooks the market stalls. Rudolph Hirt, Jr., began his business in 1887 with a stall in the old Detroit Central Market, selling eggs, butter, and cheese from local farms. But land in Cadillac Square became too valuable to be used as a farmer's market, and Hirt was one of the first to build a store in the new Eastern Market on land the city set aside in 1892.

The building still stands, and the old wooden cheese locker behind the counter is still used, although a much larger one has since been built on the second floor. The second one was needed because 40 percent of Hirt's business is selling cheese: more than 250 kinds, from well-known Swiss cheese and French brie to little-known Michigan Raw Milk Pinconning that is made in the Upper Peninsula. The shop also sells imported crackers and cookies, teas, jams, at least thirty kinds of mustards, olive oil, and other gastronomic items, all left stacked in their opened cases to make for leisurely and informal browsing. On the third floor, Hirt sells wicker baskets of all descriptions and sizes. You could purchase a basket on the third floor and then easily fill it with enough mouth-watering items on the first floor for a memorable gourmet dinner in the park.

To reach the Eastern Market head downtown on I-75 and exit east on Mack Avenue. The market is two blocks east of the expressway, near the corner of Mack and Russell avenues. R. Hirt Jr. is open Monday through Friday, 7 A.M. to 3 P.M., and Saturday, 7 A.M. to 2 P.M.

Restaurants also reflect the ethnically diverse, hard-working Detroiters who at nightfall put aside their jobs and enjoy themselves immensely with good food served in large portions at very reasonable prices.

Coney Island hotdogs and baseball are a summer tradition in the Motor City. It begins at **Tiger Stadium**, one of the oldest ballparks in the country and home of Detroit's professional baseball team. Built in 1900 and called Bennett Park, the stadium has been remodeled and renamed several times but still retains that old-fashioned atmosphere of summer baseball, where the fans feel like an extension of the game rather than passive observers. There have been attempts recently to either cover the old ballpark or build a modern domed stadium for the team, but

Detroiters rise in unison each time such proposals are made and overwhelmingly express their love for the historic structure. The Tigers (313-962-4000) play from April to September, and tickets can usually be purchased at game time at the stadium on the corner of Michigan and Trumbull avenues downtown.

To continue the tradition after the ninth inning head over to **Lafayette Coney Island**, Detroit's premier hot dog place. Located where Lafayette and Michigan avenues merge near Kennedy Square downtown, the porcelain white eatery with its male waiters is an institution in Detroit. The fare is coney dogs (with loads of chopped onions, chili, and mustard), loose burgers (loose hamburger in a hot dog bun), and bean soup served on Formica counters and tables with paper napkins and truckstop china. Yet arrive at midnight and you'll see patrons dressed in tuxedos enjoying a late-night hot dog after the symphony seated next to a couple of rabid baseball fans with their binoculars and team pennant. Lafayette Coney Island (313-964-8198) is open twenty-four hours daily with hot dogs and loose burgers priced at around $2.

Another lunch-counter restaurant downtown, **Brothers Bar-B-Q**, has the best ribs in the area. And that's saying a lot, because Detroiters take their barbecued ribs very seriously. The restaurant is located at 581 East Jefferson, across the street from the modern Renaissance Center, but it is strictly a casual down-home eatery that is consistently named the top place for spareribs by city magazines and newspapers. The ribs are actually prepared at the main Brothers Bar-B-Q on Wyoming in northwest Detroit, where they are soaked in the restaurant's own spicy "Sauce of the Islands" and then cooked on an open pit. Order a slab (or half slab for those with meek appetites), enjoy it with a mug of cold beer and a side order of Brothers's garlic coleslaw, and you have one of the best meals Detroit offers, a feast that even the city's mayor indulges in frequently. Brothers Bar-B-Q (313-963-7298) is open Monday through Thursday from 11:30 A.M. until 10 P.M., Friday from 11:30 A.M. until 11 P.M., and Saturday from 1 to 11 P.M. Ribs range from $9 to $12, and you can even take home a bottle of "Sauce of the Islands."

It may not be "off the beaten path," but Detroit's Central Automated Transit System is definitely above the city streets. Better known as the **People Mover**, the mass transit project was opened in 1987 after several years of controversial delays and cost overruns. The 2.9-mile elevated track circles the downtown heart of Detroit. Its automated cars stop every three minutes at thirteen stations, each decorated with beautiful mosaics and other art work. The ride costs only 50 cents and lasts only fourteen minutes, but it gives an excellent overall view of the city from a superb vantage point. The best stretch comes when the cars wind around Cobo Hall and passengers see a panorama of the Detroit River and the skyline of Windsor, the Canadian city to the south. The most popular stop has to be the Greektown Station, where riders pile out and head for the crowded ethnic district on Monroe Street for dinner at one of the many Greek restaurants or just a piece of baklava, dripping in honey, at the handful of bakeries there.

The People Mover (313-962-RAIL) operates from 7 A.M. until 11 P.M. Monday through Thursday and until midnight Friday, from 9 A.M. until midnight Saturday, and from noon until 8 P.M. Sunday.

The Detroit River, which connects Lake St. Clair with Lake Erie, was the avenue that the city's first residents—the French in 1701—used to arrive in Southeast Michigan. The river remains a focal point of activities for Detroiters with several parks lining its banks and one—Belle Isle—located in the middle of it. Reached by a bridge at East Jefferson and Grand River, the island park features one of the oldest municipal aquariums in the country, the **Dossin Great Lakes Museum** (313-824-3157), which traces the sailing history of the Great Lakes and has an excellent children's zoo (313-398-0900).

But a little more obscured and closer to downtown on Atwater Street is **Chene Park** with its outdoor theater, river walkway, and small pond. The delightful little park is a favorite place to wet a fishing line, enjoy a picnic, or take in one of the concerts, many of them free, that are held there throughout the summer. Call the park (313-567-0990) for dates, times, and prices of the outdoor concerts and other events it sponsors.

In 1898, a popular summer activity for Detroiters was taking a river cruise to such tourist spots as St. Clair Flats, Belle Isle, Fighting Island, and a new one known as Bois Blanc Island. The new attraction was immediately popular, but few people could pronounce the name. So it was changed to Boblo in 1908, and the company that ran the amusement park commissioned a shipyard to build two huge steamers to meet tourist demand. One was the **SS Columbia**, built in 1902, and the other was the **SS Ste. Claire**, commissioned in 1910. The four-deck boats were the largest steam-powered ferries in the world and featured huge polished dance floors inside with band stands and bars.

The two ships are still in operation today as floating national historic sites. They can carry 2,500 passengers each and depart daily from the downtown dock at the foot of Clark Avenue for the hour-and-a-half cruise to the small island 19 miles to the south. If you want to skip the amusement park but still enjoy the ships, on Friday and Saturday there are Moonlight Cruises departing at 11 P.M. with live music, dancing, and a little romancing under the stars. The ships sail—and Boblo Island (313-259-7500) is open—from May through September. Ticket prices range from $10 to $16.

The Detroit Cultural Center, located on Woodward Avenue near Wayne State University, contains the Science Center, the Detroit Historical Museum, and the Museum of African–American History. But the heart of it is the **Detroit Institute of Arts**, the one-hundred-year-old art museum that contains more than a hundred galleries, 40,000 works, and the pride of the city, the frescoes by Diego Rivera of industrial Detroit in the 1930s. A favorite way for many Detroiters to enjoy the DIA is at its "Breakfast with Bach." Offered Sunday from 10 to 11:30 A.M. year-round, the event includes a brunch of quiche, souffle, or crepes that is served in sunny Kresge Court and accompanied by chamber music. The court holds 145 people, and often the audience is a delightful mix of formally attired and casually dressed music lovers. Tickets range from $8 to $9, and reservations (313-833-7940) are recommended.

In 1975, the Michigan Department of Natural Resources opened **Maybury State Park** on an existing farm in the northwest corner of Wayne County. It was an unusual place to establish a state park, but Maybury is an unusual state park. The idea was to preserve a "living farm" close to the city so that residents, especially children, who have never experienced the sights, sounds, and, yes, smells of a working farm would have the opportunity to do so nearby. The area consists of several barns where visitors get a close, hanging-on-the-fence view of chickens, pigs, cows, goats, sheep, horses, and other typical farm animals. There is also a display of old farming equipment, but newer plows and harvesters are used by the staff who actually work the land. Kids not only get to feed the animals but view newborn chicks in the brooder room, modern tractors rumbling along, or huge draft horses pulling a plow through fields of corn, oats, beans, and other typical Michigan crops.

Also within the 1,000-acre state park are natural areas of meadows and forests with hiking trails and bike paths. A park concessionaire runs a horse stable with 8 miles of horse trails that during the winter become the destination for Nordic skiers who can rent equipment at the park. But by far the most unique aspect of Maybury is its Living Farm, which is open daily from 10 A.M. to 7 P.M. in the summer and 10 A.M. until 5 P.M. in the winter. Maybury State Park (313-349-8390) has an entrance on Eight Mile Road, 5 miles west of I-275. A vehicle fee is charged to enter the park.

Oakland County

The urban sprawl of Southeast Michigan runs its course to Pontiac, but from there the terrain changes quickly to the rolling hills, lakes, and woods of northern Oakland County. A thirty-minute drive from Detroit can remove you from the city and bring you to the doorstep of a rustic cabin on a small lake in an isolated wooded area where only foot trails pass by. **Bald Mountain Recreation Area** maintains two "frontier cabins" on the edge of Tamarack Lake that provide bunks, tables, and a wood stove for heat inside and a pit toilet and hand water pump outside. Each cabin can sleep up to twenty people, but they are rented to single parties who drive to the area and hike in the final one hundred yards. The surrounding terrain is the ridges and hills of Bald Mountain and features a network of trails and isolated lakes that offer good fishing opportunities.

The overnight rate per cabin is $44, and reservations can be made by contacting Bald Mountain Recreation Area (313-693-6767). The recreation area, which is located southeast of Lake Orion just off M-24, also has a public shooting range, a beach, picnic areas, and almost 14 miles of trails for hiking or Nordic skiing.

Farther north in Oakland County many people exit from I-75 at Grange Hall Road to explore the historic town of Holly. Established in the early 1800s, Holly was a sleepy little hamlet until 1855 when the Detroit–Milwaukee Railroad reached the town, bringing immediate growth and prosperity with the twenty-five trains that passed through daily. Martha Street near the tracks was the site of the Holly Hotel, many saloons, and frequent brawls. In 1880 there was an uproar between local rowdies and a traveling circus that left so many beaten and bruised the street became known as **Battle Alley**. The most famous moment in Battle Alley's history was on Aug. 28, 1908, when Carry A. Nation, the notorious "Kansas Saloon Smasher," arrived in Holly at the request of the local prohibition committee. The next day Nation, with umbrella in hand and her Pro-Temperance supporters a step behind her, invaded the saloons, smashing whiskey bottles, clubbing patrons, and preaching about the sins of "demon rum." Nation created the biggest flurry at the hotel, where she entered the "Dispensing Room" and attacked the painting of a nude over the bar.

Today the residents of Holly celebrate the occasion with a Carry Nation Festival the second weekend of September, highlighted by a re-enactment of that special day in 1908 along with a parade, arts and crafts booths, and much food, entertainment, and, yes, a few swigs of the very stuff Nation campaigned against. Battle Alley and its one-hundred-year-old Victorian buildings have been restored as a string of twelve specialty shops that include antique markets both along the alley and on nearby streets.

The **Holly Hotel**, which was built in 1891 and suffered through two devastating fires, the second in 1978, has since been completely restored, including the painting of the nude. It is now listed on the National Register of Historic Places but no longer provides lodging. Instead, the hotel is a fine restaurant, known for both its classic and creative cuisine, all set in a Victorian tradition that reflects its birth during the railroad era. The main dining room, with its pedestal tables, soft glow of gas lamps, and red velvet wingback chairs, is the stage for such entrees as medallions of beef with morel mushroom sauce, fillet of beef Wellington, or sauteed Michigan rainbow trout. The hotel also provides gourmet picnic baskets that include not only appetizers, dinner, desserts, and wine but also linen, flatware, candle, and a map of good picnic spots in the area.

The Holly Hotel (313-634-5208) is open for lunch Monday through Saturday from 11 A.M. until 3 P.M. and for dinner Monday through Thursday from 5 to 10 P.M., Friday and Saturday from 5 to 11 P.M., and Sunday from noon to 8 P.M. Dinner prices range from $16 to $20, and reservations are recommended.

Macomb County

Come fall one of the favorite activities in Southeast Michigan is a trip to a cider mill. Parents pack the kids in the car and head out to the edge of the county where a river turns an old wooden water wheel. The wheel is the source of power for the mill that crushes apples to extract the dark brown juice and refine it into cider, truly one of Michigan's culinary delights. After viewing the operation, visitors purchase jugs of cider, cinnamon doughnuts, and sticky caramel apples and then retreat to a place along the river. Here they enjoy a feast in the midst of brilliant fall colors, in the warmth of an Indian summer, and with the fragrance of crushed apples floating by.

Cider mills ring the metropolitan Detroit area, but one of the oldest and most colorful lies right on the border of Oakland and Macomb counties west of Rochester on Avon Road (Twenty-three Mile Road). **Yates Cider Mill** was built in 1863 along the banks of the Clinton River and began its long history as a grist mill. It has been a water-powered operation ever since, but in 1876 it began making cider and today the water wheel still powers the apple elevator, grinders, and press as well as generating electricity for the lights inside. The mill is capable of producing 300 gallons of cider per hour, all of which is needed in the fall to meet the demand of visitors who enjoy their treat around the huge red barn or across the street on the banks of the Clinton River in the Rochester–Utica State Recreation Area. Yates Cider Mill (313-651-8300) is open daily from 9 A.M. until 7 P.M. from September through November, and from noon until 5 P.M. Saturday and Sunday from December until May.

Washtenaw County

Trendy Ann Arbor, the cultural capital of Southeast Michigan (and some say the entire state), is the site of the University of Michigan, the "Harvard of the West." The university dominates the city, its buildings and campus entwined in the town's landscape. It provides many of Ann Arbor's top attractions, such as the Kelsey Museum of Archaeology, a renowned collection of art and artifacts from Egyptian, Greek, Roman, and classical Mediterranean cultures. On Saturdays in the fall Ann Arbor is U of M football; the largest stadium crowds in the country (104,000) gather to cheer the Wolverines on.

But there is a lighter side to this college town, one that children will appreciate, and it begins at the **Ann Arbor Hands-On Museum**. This is no stuffy hall with an endless row of glass-enclosed displays. The entire museum is devoted to participatory exhibits, more than eighty on four floors, and the concept that kids learn by doing. Housed in the classic Central Fire House, the museum was dedicated on Sept. 28, 1982, the one-hundredth anniversary of the building. Inside, visitors move along trying exhibits such as the sand pendular, a suspended funnel that you fill with sand and swing to make various patterns. There is also the bubble capsule, where participants step into a ring of soap film and slowly raise a cylinder bubble around them until it pops. Some exhibits use computers and deal with complex theories, others are as simple as the mystery boxes: a child sticks in a hand and attempts to guess what is touched. All the exhibits come with a printed explanation that is appreciated mostly by the parents.

The Ann Arbor Hands-on Museum (313-995-5439) is recommended for children eight years old and older. It is on the corner of Huron and Fifth Avenue, which can be reached by following Business US-23 (Main Street) from M-14 north of the city or from I-94 by exiting to US-23 and then to Washtenaw Avenue. Hours are Tuesday through Friday from 1:30 to 5:30 P.M., Saturday from 10 A.M. to 5 P.M., and Sunday from 1 to 5 P.M. There is an admission fee.

Visitors who want to shop, stroll, and dine in the atmosphere of a major university head to State Street, which borders the heart of U of M. Others head in the opposite direction to the north end of Fifth Avenue, between Kingsley and Catherine. This red brick area was part of the original village of Ann Arbor in 1824, and later the Luick Brothers built their lumber mill here. There were other nineteenth-century structures as well, including the Godfrey Warehouse which was constructed in 1899. By the 1960s all were destined for the wrecking ball when a campaign began to save them. What has evolved is the **Kerrytown Shops**.

Three buildings, including the Luick and Godfrey structures, were restored and connected to each other with elevated walkways to make a shopping complex that now houses thirty-five open-air shops, one blending into the next. It is a delightful assortment of cafes, markets, specialty shops, and small outdoor courtyards, where you find everything from a fresh-baked croissant and a homemade rocking horse to imported crayfish and squid at Monahan's Seafood. One of the larger shops, and one of the more interesting from a cook's point of view, is the Kitchen Port (313-665-9188), a well-stocked cooking store that offers classes and clinics throughout the year. A lunch of croissant sandwiches, pasta salads, or quiche can be enjoyed at the Moveable Feast, the original restaurant. (A second restaurant by this name is located at 326 W. Liberty and today is regarded by many as Ann Arbor's finest.) Next door to Kerrytown is the Ann Arbor Farmers Market. Visit this area when the market is open and the farmers have filled its stalls with crates of fresh produce (Wednesday and Saturday from May through December, Saturday only during the rest of the year) and you easily have Ann Arbor's most delightful shopping experience.

St. Clair County

The county is often referred to as the Blue Water region of Michigan as it is bounded by Lake St. Clair to the south, Lake Huron to the north, and the St. Clair River to the east. M-29 circles the north side of Lake St. Clair and then follows the river to Port Huron, passing small towns and many bait shops, marinas, and shoreline taverns advertising walleye and perch fish fries. The most charming town on the water is St. Clair, 15 miles south of Port Huron and a major shipbuilding center in the early 1900s. The city recently renovated its downtown section, centering it on **Riverwalk Park**, which residents claim is the longest boardwalk in the world facing fresh water. The favorite activity on the 1,500-foot riverwalk is to watch the Great Lake freighters that glide by exceptionally close, giving land-bound viewers a good look at the massive boats and their crews. The second-favorite activity is walleye fishing. The St. Clair River is renowned for this fish, and anglers can be seen throughout the summer tossing a line from the riverwalk, trying to entice the walleye with minnows or nightcrawlers.

Above the walkway is a wide, grassy bank filled with sunbathers, kids playing, and in mid-June the arts and crafts booths of the St. Clair Art Fair, a popular festival along the river. Call the St. Clair Chamber of Commerce (313-329-3366) for the exact dates and times. The riverwalk ends to the north at the Saint Clair Inn, a historic hotel that features outdoor dining in a courtyard overlooking the river.

Port Huron, a city of 30,000, is the site of the Bluewater Bridge, the international crossing between Michigan and Sarnia, Ontario. It is also recognized throughout the state as the start of the Port Huron–Mackinac Sailboat Race in late July. On the eve of the

The Victorian Inn in Port Huron

event, known as **Boat Night**, the downtown area of Water, Lapeer, and Quay streets, which border the docks on Black River, become congested block parties. Sailors, local people, and tourists mingle in a festival that spreads throughout the streets, the yacht clubs, and even on the sailboats themselves.

On the quieter side is the historical aspect of Port Huron with its many stately homes, one of which has been renovated into **The Victorian Inn**. Located at 1229 Seventh Street in a neighborhood of nineteenth-century mansions, the home was built in 1896 by James Davidson, who owned a dry goods company in town. Two families purchased the home in 1983 and turned it into a fine restaurant on the main floor, a pub in the basement, and a place of lodging upstairs. Listed on the State Register of Historic Places, the home is an excellent example of nineteenth-century craftsmanship with its hand-carved oak woodwork, leaded-glass windows, and plasterwork and trim on the ceilings. The patrons enjoy their meals in one of three small rooms that make up the dining area, one with a massive fireplace. The menu changes every month but generally features entrees of beef, fish, and chicken and includes full explanations of every dish served. The dinners are excellent, the dessert tray beyond the will power of most people.

The restaurant (313-984-1437) is open Tuesday through Saturday from 11:30 A.M. until 2 P.M. for lunch and from 6 to 10 P.M. for dinner. Evening entrees range from $15 to $20, while lodging upstairs is $45 to $60, depending on the room, for double occupancy.

A short walk from the Victorian Inn is the **Port Huron Museum of Arts and History** (313-982-0891) at 1115 Sixth Street. The museum combines an art gallery with collections of natural history and artifacts from Port Huron's past. Included are bones and displays of the prehistoric mammoths that roamed Michigan's Thumb 10,000 years ago and memorabilia of Thomas Edison's boyhood home which was located in the city. A popular attraction is the reconstructed pilot house of a Great Lake freighter. All the furnishings were taken from various ships, and visitors can work the wheel, signal the alarm horn, or ring the engine bell. All around the pilot house is a huge mural that gives the impression you are guiding the vessel into Lake Huron. The museum (313-982-0891), housed in a 1904 Carnegie library, is open Wednesday through Saturday from 1 to 4:30 P.M. There is no admission.

Monroe County

General George Armstrong Custer may have staged his ill-fated "Last Stand" at Little Bighorn in Montana, but he grew up in Monroe, Michigan. Custer was actually born in Rumley, Ohio, but spent most of his youth, until he entered a military academy at the age of sixteen, living with his half sister in this city along Lake Erie. Even after he became a noted brigadier general during the Civil War, Custer continued to return to Monroe, and in 1864 he married Elizabeth Bacon, his boyhood sweetheart here.

Custer's intriguing life can be traced at the **Monroe County Historical Museum**, which features the largest collection of the general's personal artifacts in the country. The Custer exhibit room occupies a fourth of the museum floor and focuses on his youth in Monroe and his distinguished Civil War career rather than his well-known days on the Western plains. There is an overcoat of buffalo hide that he wore during a winter campaign in 1868 and a buckskin suit that is impressive with its beadwork and porcupine quills. Custer was an avid outdoorsman and also a fine taxidermist. It comes as a surprise to many that Custer enjoyed mounting the game animals he hunted, but housed in the museum is his favorite Remington buffalo rifle along with many mounted game animals.

The museum also has displays on Monroe's early history, which dates back to French missionaries in 1634, and on the famous Battle of River Raisin in 1813. But it is the life and tragic death of General Custer that most people find fascinating. The Monroe County Historical Museum (313-243-7137) is at 126 South Monroe Street in the heart of the city and open from Wednesday through Sunday from 10 A.M. to 5 P.M. During the summer it is also open on Tuesday. There is no admission fee.

Off the Beaten Path in The Thumb

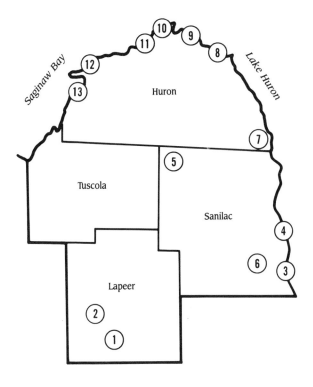

1. Metamora/White Horse Inn/ Metamora Hunt Club
2. Lapeer/Lapeer County Courthouse/Past Tense Country Store
3. Lexington/Charles H. Moore Library/Governor's Inn
4. Port Sanilac/Loop-Harrison House Museum/The Raymond Inn/Bellaire Hotel
5. Petroglyphs State Historical Park
6. Coswell/Coswell Berry Farm
7. White Rock/School House Museum

8. Huron City/Huron City Museum/ Lighthouse County Park
9. Grindstone/Grindstone Bar and Grill
10. Port Austin/Garfield Inn/Lake Street Manor/The Bank 1884
11. Port Crescent State Park
12. Caseville/Hamrick's Resort Perch Charters
13. Bay Port/Bay Port Fish Co./ Mrs. Zebbie's Fish Kitchen

The Thumb

Within the mitten that is the lower peninsula of Michigan there is a special area known as the "Thumb." The state's most recognized appendage is shaped by Saginaw Bay to the west and Lake Huron to the east. The bodies of water not only outline the peninsula but have wrapped it in rural isolation, the Thumb's trademark and the reason it is called "the getaway close to home."

Home is likely to be one of three of the state's largest urban areas: Detroit, Flint, or Saginaw, all less than a two-hour drive from the four counties that compose the region. Yet the Thumb is a world away. In this place where interstate highways give way to country roads and indistinguishable suburbs turn into distinct villages, the bustle and heartbeat of the city is replaced by the rural charm of the country.

You don't have nightclubs in the Thumb or dominating skylines or symphony orchestras. But you have more than 90 miles of lake shore to view, small museums to discover, and an easy way of life whose rural pace will soothe the soul and rest a weary urban mind.

Lumber companies opened up the Thumb in the early 1800s, but after the trees were gone and the loggers had departed north, the region slipped into the small-town realm of agriculture. Today the area is still predominantly a farm belt, and from its rich soil come corn, sugar beets, grains, beans, and the lush grass that supports vast dairy herds and livestock. Huron County, alone, produces the most navy beans per acre in the world.

In recent years, tourist dollars have become a significant part of the economy, but the region will never turn into one of the strips of motels and ice cream stands that characterize much of the Lake Michigan shoreline, the heart of the Michigan tourism. The Thumb lies on the other side of the state, away from the mainstream of summer traffic. And many travelers, who come for the fine beaches, country markets and picturesque lighthouses, leave it cherishing that out-of-the-way character the most.

Lapeer County

A common misconception of the Thumb held by many Michigan natives is that the region is flat, without so much as a ripple between the shoreline of Saginaw Bay and the lapping waters of

Lake Huron. A drive through Lapeer County dispels that notion immediately. The rolling hills that are the trademark of northern Oakland County continue north through the heart of the peninsula. In southern Lapeer County, these hills have an enhancement that makes them unique in Michigan: the distinct white rail fences of horse country. Follow County Road 62 between M-24 and M-53 and dip south along the gravel crossroads of Blood, Garder, or Barber, and you'll pass through one of the greatest concentrations of horse farms in the state. Come in late spring when the grass is green, a new coat of whitewash covers the fences, and the mares and foals are trotting through the fields . . . and this area could easily be mistaken for the bluegrass region of Kentucky.

The heart of Michigan's horse country is Metamora, a small village of 500 that lies just east of M-24 and is crowned by the towering steeple of the Pilgrim Church (built in 1878). Settlers first began arriving in the area in 1838, but Metamora earned a spot on the map when it became a stop for a stagecoach route that later turned into the Detroit–Bay City Railroad in 1872. Whether travelers were carried by horse or by rail, the resting place was the same: a large rambling carriage house built in 1850 on one corner of County Road 62 and Metamora Road.

Back then it was known as the Hoard House after its proprietor Lorenzo Hoard who charged travelers, weary from a long day on the carriage, only 50 cents a room. Today it's called the **White Horse Inn**, and while they no longer have rooms for rent, they are still serving meals 137 years later, making it the oldest operating restaurant in the county. One half of the inn is the dining room, completely sealed off from the barnlike barroom, and decorated in dark oak, leaded-glass windows, and red plaid carpeting. On Thursdays both halves are filled with customers as the inn offers its weekly all-you-can-consume fish fry for $4 per person. But the rest of its menu is equally tempting, especially its White Horse Wellington, a flaky pastry filled with tenderloin, mushrooms, and cheese. The inn also has a list of daily seafood specials such as Rainbow Trout a la Praline, boneless trout dusted with a seasoned flour and sauteed in butter with pecans.

The White Horse Inn (313-678-2150) is open Monday through Thursday from 11 A.M. until midnight, Friday and Saturday from 11 A.M. until 2 P.M., and Sunday from 2 P.M. until midnight. Menu prices range from $7 to $13 for dinners, $2 to $4 for lunch; reservations are recommended on the weekends.

Many think the horse farms can trace their origins back to the

21

Metamora Hunt Club which began in 1928. The club was established by wealthy riders from Grosse Pointe and Bloomfield Hills whose own wooded areas were lost to the growing urbanization of Detroit. The riders were looking for a new place to pursue their old English fox hunts, and around Metamora they found a perfect setting: a terrain of rolling hills, scattered lakes, and wooded acres.

The hunt club still meets three times a week for its fox hunts, and the area now supports thriving house farms known for their thoroughbreds, Arabians, and quarter horses. The season for the fox hunts runs from mid-August through January. Hunts begin at sunrise when the riders, who arrive dressed in top hats, "pink" coats (that are really red), and other traditional garb, enjoy a glass of sherry. They then mount their horses at the sound of bugles and follow a pack of fox hounds through the woods and fields until the wily fox loses his large group of pursuers.

The hunts last two to four hours, and spectators are welcome to watch the festivities at the beginning. They are held Monday, Wednesday, and Saturday, beginning at different horse farms in the area. Two of the more spectacular hunts ar held on Thanksgiving morning and around the first Saturday of October when the club celebrates its "Blessing of the Hounds." Either hunt may draw more than seventy riders and an equal number of spectators. There is no charge to watch the hunts, and locations and times can be obtained by calling the Hunt Club Kennels (313-678-2711).

North of Metamora along M-24 is Lapeer, a town of 6,270 and the county seat. Settlers began arriving in the area in 1828 and borrowed their village name from "la pierre," the French translation of the Indian name for Flint River, which lies nearby. Lapeer became the county seat in 1831, and eight years later the county courthouse was built in the town common.

Lapeer is still the center of government and the **County Courthouse** still stands at the corner of Court and Nepessing streets. It is an impressive building, featuring a Greek Revival style with four fluted Doric columns. It's topped by a three-tiered tower and a Roman dome and is noted as the "oldest courthouse still being used in Michigan today," even though the county has long since built a newer, all-brick building across the street. But the old courthouse keeps its title because every summer the judge, the jury, and a handful of history buffs move to the other side of the street to hear a few cases in the second-floor courtroom of this landmark structure.

Lapeer County Courthouse in Lapeer

The first floor is now the Lapeer Historical Society Museum, and for a small admission fee, visitors can wander through the turn-of-the-century judge's chambers or the first sheriff's office in the county. The Courthouse Museum is open from early June until Nov. 15. Hours are 1 to 5 P.M. Tuesday through Friday.

More history and a lot of country charm can be found just up the road from Lapeer at the **Past Tense Country Store**. The store is only minutes from downtown Lapeer and can be reached by driving north on M-24 and then turning east on County Road 7 (Daley Road). The first intersection on Daley is Farnsworth Road, and visible to the south from this intersection is one of the most impressive houses in the region. The huge, twenty-three–room home was built by the Farnsworth family, who were part of the first wave of settlers to farm the county. There are several buildings on the old farm, including the original barn that Lucie Hiner renovated into the Past Tense Country Store in 1971.

The store is an intriguing place, worth browsing through even if you are not in a buying mood. It is part country store, part antique shop, and part museum. Walk in on a chilly day and the rush of warm air from the wood-burning stove greets you. Then you'll notice the one-hundred-year-old German barrel piano and the classic red Texaco gasoline pump next to it. The store itself is four separate rooms, each stocked to the rafters with such items as handmade baskets, dried flowers, candles, knickknacks, and children's toys, including one of the most amazing teddy bear collections you'll ever see outside a museum. Upstairs are numerous pieces of antique furniture, while one room is devoted to Christmas with an old sled in the middle and walls covered with ornaments.

But between every shelf of merchandise, Hiner draws you back into the rural history of Lapeer with small artifacts she has saved. Above the wall of hard candy, a requirement in every country store, are rows of cleaning products and cans of food, all from an era long gone. Some you'll recognize, like Oxydol, Quaker Oats, or Calumet Baking Powder, though the packaging hardly resembles the modern-day counterparts. Many you will not (Quick Arrow Soup Chips or Red Moon Early Peas), for they have long since vanished from supermarkets.

Hiner and her family live in the Farnsworth house and operate the store, which is open Monday through Saturday from 10 A.M. until 6 P.M. and Sunday from noon to 6 P.M.

Sanilac County

M-25, the state road that leads out of Port Huron, follows the shoreline of Sanilac County and continues along the entire coast of the Thumb, ending in Bay City. While the road does not offer a watery view at every bend, there are more than enough panoramas of Lake Huron and shoreline parks to make it one of the more scenic drives in the Lower Peninsula.

Heading north on M-25, the first town you reach in Sanilac County is Lexington, which was incorporated in 1855 and boomed at the turn of the century. Back then the bustling town of 2,400 was a common stop for Great Lakes shipping and boasted an organ factory, a brewery, a flour mill, and six saloons. But the great storm of 1913 that swept across Lake Huron destroyed the town's shipping docks and virtually isolated it. Lexington slipped into a standstill until the automobile and roads revived it in the

1940s, and today the town of almost 800 has worked harder than any other community in the Thumb to promote its future by preserving its past.

Lexington's streets are lined with turn-of-the-century homes and buildings, including four that are listed on the National Register of Historic Places. One of them is the **Charles H. Moore Public Library** at the corner of Main and Huron streets next to village hall. The brick building was built in 1859 as the Devine Law Office but somehow passed into the hands of Moore, a local seaman who died in 1901, leaving the building to his three daughters. When a dispute erupted in 1903 as to where to put the town library, the daughters offered the former law office as a permanent site.

It has been the library ever since and today holds almost 12,000 books, including a rare book collection. But librarians will tell you that as many people wander through just to view the renovated interior as to check out a book. The wood trim and stained-glass windows have been fully restored inside, as has the graceful wooden bannister that leads you past a picture of the "old seaman" to the upstairs. It's hard to imagine a more pleasant place to read than the sunlit room on the second floor, which features desks, tables, and office chairs that were originally used by the law firm.

The Moore Library (313-359-8267) is open Monday from 5 to 8 P.M.., Wednesday and Friday from 10:30 A.M. to 5 P.M., and Saturday from 11 A.M. to 3 P.M.

Moore was also responsible for another building in Lexington that is known as a National Historic Site. When the seaman built his home sometime in the 1880s, he purposely chose to locate it just a block from the lake where he plied his trade. The huge Queen Anne–style home on the corner of Simmon and Washington streets was constructed from white pine that loggers were shipping out of the port of Lexington. In 1901, Mary, the youngest daughter, used the house as a backdrop for her marriage to Albert E. Sleeper, a newly elected state senator. When Sleeper's political career led to his election as governor in 1917, the house became an important summer retreat for the couple, who were eager to escape the busy public life in Lansing.

Today the home is still used as a summer retreat. Bob and Jane McDonald purchased it in 1982 and the next year opened it up as the **Governor's Inn**, Lexington's first bed and breakfast. Although they gave it a new name and a fresh coat of paint, not

25

much else has changed; it is easy to slip back to the early 1900s while staying at this inn. The three guestrooms upstairs are furnished with iron beds, Haywood-Wakefield wicker, and lace curtains that are draped across the nearly floor-to-ceiling windows. Guests spend summer evenings much the same way the governor and his wife did—on the wraparound porch in wicker rockers (there are seven now instead of two) enjoying the cool breezes off Lake Huron.

The double bedrooms (private baths) are $30 per night. Reservations are recommended and can be made by writing Governor's Inn, P.O. Box 471, Lexington, MI 48450, or by phone (313-359-5770).

From Lexington, M-25 continues north along the Lake Huron shoreline and in 11 miles reaches the next lakeside town. Port Sanilac began in the 1830s as a group of crude shanties for lumbermen and was known as Bark Shanty Point until residents decided in 1857 that the name of a famous Wyandotte Indian chief was a little more dignified for their community.

The town's most distinctive landmark is the Port Sanilac Lighthouse with its red brick house and whitewashed tower overlooking the town harbor and watery horizon of Lake Huron. But like Lexington, Port Sanilac's early history and wealth can be seen in the old homes that border its streets. One is the **Loop-Harrison House**, a huge Victorian mansion just south of town on M-25. The home was built in 1872 by Dr. Joseph Loop, who arrived in Sanilac in 1854 and began a practice that covered a 40-mile radius. The home and its immense furnishings passed down through three generations of the family until Captain Stanley Harrison, grandson of the good doctor, donated it to the Sanilac Historical Society in 1964.

The Historical Society has kept the home intact and visitors can wander through two floors of rooms that have remained virtually the same since the 1870s, right down to the original carpet, cooking utensils in the kitchen, and the doctor's instruments in his office. There is also a dairy museum out back and a furnished 1882 pioneer log cabin. The Loop-Harrison House is open from mid-June through Labor Day from 11 A.M. until 4:30 P.M. There is a small admission fee.

Closer to town on M-25 is another impressive home that has become **The Raymond House Inn**, Port Sanilac's bed and breakfast. The home was built in 1871 by Uri Raymond, one of the founding fathers of the town, who established what is now Michigan's oldest continuously operating hardware store just up the street. The exterior of this Victorian-style home makes it hard to miss with its red brick facade, high peaked roofs, and white gingerbread trim. Inside, high ceilings, classic moldings, winding staircases, and large rooms add to the turn-of-the-century charm of the inn.

Shirley Denison bought the house after three generations of Raymonds had lived in it. Denison is a restorative artist from Washington, D.C., but she spent her childhood summers in Port Sanilac where her grandfather was a local boat and lumber baron. She was enchanted by the antique furniture that filled the rooms, including the old-fashioned parlor and the six bedrooms she rents out on the second floor. The third floor she turned into an antique shop, while in the rear of the house she has an art gallery filled with her sculpture and pottery and work from other local artists. There are also bicycles available for guests.

The inn is open from May through October with a rate of $45 for double occupancy (private bath). Write to Denison at 111 South Ridge Street, Port Sanilac, MI 48469, or call (313-622-8800) for a room reservation.

For dinner or what many say is the best fish fry in the Thumb, head almost directly across the street to yet another century-old Victorian home known as the **Bellaire Hotel**. Inside you'll find more arches, ceiling-high windows, and parquet floors. More important to the patrons, however, are the dining rooms and what emerges from the kitchen. Local people call them "porch dinners," for you sit in a glass-enclosed room overlooking the gardens that surround the hotel. Diane Douros, who has operated the Bellaire since she and her husband bought it in 1945, is best known for her perch and pickerel dinners. The meal is complete only if it is topped off with a piece of her tart lemon meringue pie. The Bellaire (313-622-9981) is at 120 South Ridge Road, and its entrees are priced from $8 to $11.

The stretch of M-25 from Port Sanilac to Forestville is especially scenic and passes three roadside parks on high bluffs from which you can scramble to the Lake Huron shoreline below. But for those who want to explore the center of the Thumb, the Bay City–Forestville Road, the only intersection in tiny Forestville, provides a good excuse to turn off M-25.

Head west on the road, through the hamlets of Charleston and

Minden, and look for the "petroglyphs" sign at the corner of Bay City–Forestville and Germania roads. **Petroglyphs State Historical Park** is located just south on Germania and is marked by a large Department of Natural Resources sign. Located in the wooded heart of the Thumb, the park features a large slab of stone with petroglyphs, Indian carvings that archaeologists believe to be between 300 and 1,000 years old and the only ones in the Lower Peninsula. The DNR has erected a large pavilion over the rock, which contains dozens of carvings. The most prominent one features a bowman with a single long line depicting his arm and arrow. There is no entrance fee. A short trail leads from the parking lot a few hundred yards inland to the pavilion.

Another reason to head inland in summer and fall is to pick berries—sweet, juicy, and back-breakingly close to the ground. Next to the town of Coswell is the **Coswell Berry Farm** (313-679-3273) at 33 Black River Road. This farm features strawberries from June to early July and then extends the picking season with blueberries and finishes up the year with raspberries that are harvested as late as November. Hours are 7 A.M. until 6 P.M. Monday through Saturday and 7 A.M. until 4 P.M. Sunday.

Huron County

The country charm of M-25 continues into Huron County as it winds north toward Port Austin on the "tip of the Thumb." Along the way it passes **White Rock School Museum**, located right off M-25 on White Rock Road. The one-room schoolhouse was built in 1909 and used for students in kindergarten through eighth grade until 1968. Today it houses many of the original books, desks, and charts that most other schools did away with at the turn of the century. There is also a restored horse barn nearby where the teacher kept her carriage. The museum has sporadic hours, but you can call J. Schroeder (517–864–5532) for a delightful tour and story of the school, or better yet stop in on the first Saturday in August when all of White Rock gathers for its annual, old-fashioned "Pot-Luck" at the schoolhouse. Make sure you bring a dish of your favorite food.

Another small museum is located 25 miles north just off M-25 on Lighthouse Road in **Lighthouse County Park**. It's in the first floor of the classic lighthouse, which was built in 1857 and is still used by the U.S. Coast Guard to guide ships. The lighthouse actually overlooks two parks; the county park around it features seventy-four campsites with electricity for recreational vehicles, a swimming beach, a boat launch, and a picnic area. But out in Lake Huron is an underwater park, the Thumb Area Bottomland Preserve, that the state set up in 1985 to protect the nine known shipwrecks that lie offshore. Relics gathered from the wrecks will be stored in the Lighthouse Museum, which is open weekends during the summer. There is no admission for the park or museum.

Where Lighthouse Road loops back to M-25 is the Thumb's most impressive attraction, **Huron City**. The town was founded in the mid-1850s by lumberman Langdon Hubbard, who needed a port for his 29,000-acre tract of timberlands that included most of northern Huron County. It quickly became the largest town in the county with several hundred residents and two sawmills that produced 80,000 feet of lumber a day. But the Great Fire of 1881 that swept across the Thumb devastated Hubbard's logging efforts. The lumber baron sold his land to immigrant farmers (after opening a bank to lend them the money), and for a while Huron City hung on as a farming community.

After withering away to a ghost town by the early 1900s, the area experienced a revival—a religious awakening, you might say—when one of Hubbard's daughters married William Lyon Phelps, a Yale professor and an ordained minister. Each summer the couple returned to Huron City and stayed at Seven Gables, the rambling Hubbard home, and eventually Dr. Phelps began preaching in the nearby church on Sunday. Local people soon discovered the magic of his oratory: simple solutions and relief from the problems of everyday life. The church that originally held 250 was quickly enlarged to 1,000 in the 1920s as people throughout Michigan heard of the preacher and began finding their way to Huron City for sunday afternoon service.

Dr. Phelps died in 1937, but Huron City survived when the granddaughter of the founder preserved the community as a museum town. There are twelve buildings on the site, nine of them furnished and open to the public. They include a country store, the church, a lifesaving station, a settler's cabin, the old inn, a barn with antique farm equipment, and the Phelps Museum which was built in honor of the minister in the early 1950s. Huron City (517-428-4123) is open July 1 through Labor Day, and the admission fee into the town includes an hour-long guided tour through the buildings that tells the stories behind them.

At this point M-25 begins to curve around the top of the Thumb, quickly passing a spur road to Grindstone City, which is named after the huge grindstones, some 6 feet in diameter, left on the beach from the days when this tiny town and its abundance of natural sandstone produced most of the world's grinding wheels. For an oral history of the era and the best hamburger in the Thumb, see Joe Mazzoni at the **Grindstone Bar And Grill** (517-738-7665) on Point Aux Barques Road near the public boat ramp. The resaurant is open from May through October for lunch and dinner.

Where Lake Huron and Saginaw Bay meet is Port Austin, the town at the "Tip of the Thumb." M-25 winds through the center of Port Austin and near its two busiest spots in the summer, the city marina and, just east of the marina's breakwall, delightful Bird Creek Park with its boardwalk and sandy beach where people gather nightly to watch the sunset over Saginaw Bay. Travelers will find some unique accommodations in this New England–style town that boomed with lumber barons in the mid-1800s.

One of them is the **Garfield Inn**, a huge, red mansion on Lake Street that is named after a U.S. congressman who stayed in the home in the 1860s and once delivered a stirring speech from its balcony endorsing Civil War hero Ulysses Grant for president. That man was James Garfield, who later became the twentieth president of the United States. The home eventually fell into the hands of Gary and Gayle Regnier, who worked for two years restoring it before opening it up in 1985 as an inn, restaurant, and bar. The inn has been named a national historic site and among its more striking features is the mahogany bar and the winding cherry wood staircase that leads to the ten bedrooms upstairs of which seven are rented out.

The Garfield Inn (517-738-5254) is open from the middle of April until January. Rooms based on double occupancy run from $65 to $75 for the one that Garfield himself used and include breakfast and a bottle of champagne. The restaurant opens at 11 A.M. daily for lunch and dinner with entree prices that range from $10 to $20.

Almost across the street is **Lake Street Manor**, a red brick home with a high peaked roof and gingerbread trim built in 1884 by another lumber baron. Carolyn Greenwood acquired the home, including much of the original furniture, from its fourth owner in 1986 and promptly opened it up as a bed and breakfast, renting out two rooms with private baths and two rooms with a shared bath. Downstairs in the Gas Light Room, Greenwood serves continental breakfast to all her guests. They can also wander into the Bay Room for a soak in a large hot tub that sits in front of a fireplace and overlooks the fenced-in Victorian gardens that she has landscaped in the back. Greenwood also has bicycles for those who want to pedal around Port Austin. The Lake Street Manor (517-738-7720) is open year-round, and room rates range from $40 to $55.

In keeping with the restored atmosphere of the Port Austin's inns, there is **The Bank 1884** restaurant for, unquestionably, the finest dining in town. Built in 1884 as the Winsorsnover Bank on the corner of Lake and State streets, the red-washed brick building ceased being a place of financial business in 1957. In 1982, Anthony and Marilynne Berry began renovating the building, and two years later they opened its doors as a restaurant. The interior features stained-glass over the classic stand-up bar, a teller's cage on the first floor, and walls of oversized photographs depicting early Huron County. The changing menu usually has shrimp scampi, prime rib, and En Papelote, walleye that is prepared with a crab meat dressing and baked in parchment paper. The Bank 1884 is open daily during the summer except Monday from 5 to 10:30 P.M. and weekends during May and after Labor Day until Nov. 1. Prices for entrees range from $9 to $17, and reservations (517-738-5353) are strongly recommended for the weekends.

West of Port Austin, M-25 begins to follow the shoreline of Saginaw Bay and is especially scenic in its 19-mile stretch to Caseville. It passes many views of the Bay and its islands, numerous roadside parks, and the finest beaches in the Thumb. One of the parks is **Port Crescent State Park**, popular with sunbathers and swimmers for the long stretches of sandy shoreline. But the park also offers opportunities and facilities for camping, hiking, and fishing, and it contains the Thumb's only set of dunes, a unique place for beachcombers to explore. There is an entrance fee to Port Crescent State Park (517-738-8663) and an $ 8 charge to camp overnight.

Even more than for sand and sun, Saginaw Bay has always been known as an angler's destination for yellow perch. Visitors, especially families, without a boat or knowledge of where to go can still enjoy good fishing by joining a perch party boat. The large charter boats hold between twenty and forty anglers and usually depart twice a day for half-day fishing trips. In Caseville, **Hamrick's Resort** (517-856-2323), a marina at 6545 Riverside, offers party boat charters that depart at 7:30 A.M. and 1:30 P.M. daily. The fee is $10 per angler. You need to bring your pole; they provide the bait and take you where the perch are biting. Perch fishing is easy, and on a good day you may need a bucket to bring home your catch.

To enjoy your perch without having to put a minnow on your hook, stay on M-25 as it curves southwest toward Bay Port. From the 1880s until the late 1940s, this sleepy village was known as the "largest freshwater fishing port in the world," as tons of perch, whitefish, walleye, and herring were shipped as far away as New York City and Chicago in refrigerated railroad cars. Today it honors its fishing past on the first Sunday in August with its annual Bay Port Fish Sandwich Day. The small festival includes arts, crafts, softball games, and lots of sandwiches—close to 8,000 are served during the event.

There is still a small commercial fishery operating in Bay Port, a place to go for fresh walleye, perch, whitefish, and herring. From the center of town head for the waterfront docks of the **Bay Port Fish Co.** (517-656-2121) for the catch of the day or to watch fishermen work on the boats or nets in the evening. The company, which is open from 9 A.M. until 5 P.M. daily, also sells smoked fish.

Finally, those who want nothing to do with catching, cleaning, or cooking their perch should head to **Mrs. Zebbie's Fish Kitchen** (517-656-7171), located right on M-25 in Bay Port. Mrs. Zebbie's serves excellent fish sandwiches (perch, walleye, or herring) or entire dinners that range from $3 to $6. It's all carry-out service, because the rest of the store is a bait and tackle shop.

Off the Beaten Path in Lake Huron

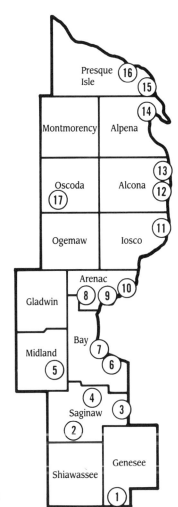

1. Balloon Corporation of America in Fenton
2. Heritage House in Chesaning
3. Frankenmuth/G. Heileman Brewing Company/The Tiffany Biergarten
4. The Temple Theatre in Saginaw
5. Tridge in Midland
6. Bay City/Bay City City Hall
7. Capt'n Jack's Landing
8. Iva's in Sterling
9. Point Au Gres Hotel
10. Singing Bridge
11. Sawyer Canoe Company in Oscoda
12. Cedar Brook Trout Farm
13. Sturgeon Point Lifesaving Station
14. The Country Cupboard in Alpena
15. Besser Natural Area
16. Fireside Inn on Grand Lake
17. Kirtland's Warbler Tours in Mio

Lake Huron

The Lake Huron shoreline, the eastern side of Michigan, is a region that has gone full circle in its history and its appearance. The first inhabitants of the area were Indians who traveled lightly through the woods and lived off the land but rarely disfigured it. When Europeans arrived they were awed by what was perceived as an endless forest, woods so thick with towering white pines that the sun rarely reached the forest floor.

All that changed in the mid-1800s. Lumbering companies that had exhausted the forest in Maine were looking for pine to cut for new settlements on the Great Plains, which were desperate for wood in their treeless region. Michigan met those needs as the greatest lumber-producing state in the nation between 1850 and 1910 with an estimated 700 logging camps and more than 2,000 mills. Massive log drives filled the Saginaw and Au Sable rivers, which were avenues to the sawmill towns on Lake Huron. In milltowns like Saginaw and Bay City, sawmills lined the riverbanks, and huge mansions lined the streets as more wealth was made off Michigan's white pine than by miners in the Klondike gold rush.

But by the turn of the century, all that was left were the stumps. The lumbering era had devastated the region, turning it into treeless areas that were wastelands of soil erosion. The Huron National Forest was established in 1909 along the Au Sable River, the first of many such preserves, in an effort to repair and manage the land. Lake Huron entered a new era when words like reforestation, conservation, and renewable resources replaced the lumbering lingo of log drives, river rats, and clearcuts.

Almost a century later the northeastern portion of the Lower Peninsula is once again a forested region. The trees are of a different generation and often a different species, but the effect on visitors is the same as when the first Europeans wandered through. To walk quietly among the towering pines in a forest padded by needles while listening to the gentle rustling of a cold-water trout stream is as much an attraction in this part of the state as sandy beaches or a cottage on the lake.

Genesee County

The heart of this county is Flint, Michigan's fourth-largest city, but the edge of it is country with rolling farms and small towns. One of the towns is Fenton, and located outside it, among the fields and pastures, is the **Balloon Corporation of America**. The business began in 1972 when several balloonists joined together and used their hot-air devices to spread word about their favorite candidate. The advertising was so unique that they quickly became swamped with similar requests from other businesses. They incorporated and in 1984 built their present office and balloon-port in the rural area north of Fenton where dozens of nearby lakes provide excellent scenery from above.

The company is involved in many things, importing balloons from England, handling promotional needs, and even running a balloon camp with hands-on instruction for new balloonists. But it's most noted as the place to go for a hot-air balloon ride. The rides are offered twice a day either at 5:30 A.M. or 7 P.M. when there is the least amount of wind turbulence. Time in the air is forty-five to sixty minutes, but the entire flight lasts almost three hours, including pre-flight preparation and pickup after landing. Although the pilot raises the balloon from ground level to around 1,000 feet, much of the flying is done right above tree level, and riders discover the wicker basket to be surprisingly stable with little sensational movement. There are a number of different flights—fall color tours, winter flights, Bed-Breakfast-and-Ballooning—but all end with a traditional champagne celebration upon landing.

Balloon Corporation of America (313-629-0040) is located at 2084 Thompson Road, which can be reached from US-23. Balloon rides are $135 per person, and reservations three weeks in advance are needed for weekend flights in the summer. A week's notice is sufficient for weekday flights.

Saginaw County

The only Michigan county without a natural lake has plenty of water as the Saginaw, Tittabawassee, Bad, Cass, Shiawassee, and Flint rivers make it the largest river basin in the state with 160 miles of waterway. It was these natural avenues and the vast forests bordering them that allowed the area to boom with loggers and sawmills in the mid-1800s. By the early 1900s the trees and loggers were gone, but reminders of the immense wealth they produced are seen throughout the county in magnificent Victorian-era homes, especially along the Boulevard in Chesaning, a major lumbering center on the Shiawassee River in the southwest corner of the county.

The Boulevard (part of M-57) and its historic homes were developed into the Old Home Shoppes, seven of the houses that are now gift and antique shops. But the beginning and the heart of it is the **Chesaning Heritage House**, one of the finest restaurants in Saginaw County. The house was built in 1908 by George Nanson as a monument to his family's lumbering business. Nanson's father, Robert, was born in England but arrived in 1852 in Chesaning, where he began as a farmer but ended up building a sawmill and, true to the American dream, became one of the wealthiest persons in the lumber town. The Georgian Revival–style house reflects all this with stately Ionic columns outside and the grand rotunda opening between the first and second floors inside.

The house changed hands a few times and was even vacant for ten years before Howard and Bonnie Ebenhoeh purchased it and opened up the restaurant in 1980. Dining is a leisurely affair in one of seven rooms on the first or second floor. Four of the rooms have fireplaces that are lit during the winter; another room is the original sun porch, now a glass-enclosed terrace that holds a half dozen tables. The Heritage House prides itself in the preparation of Michigan beef, and one of its specialties is baked tenderloin for two, which arrives with a crown of mushrooms. The dessert tray is also deliciously tempting and always includes an ice cream sundae pie.

The Heritage House (517-845-7700) is open daily from 11 A.M. until 9:30 P.M. and Sunday from noon until 9 P.M. Dinners range from $9 to $17. Behind the restaurant, the original carriage house has been turned into an antique and gift shop with two floors of furniture, crafts, dolls, and a 1908 horse carriage on display upstairs.

Generally recognized as Michigan's number one attraction is the German town of Frankenmuth. "Little Bavaria" is famous for home-style chicken dinners served at one of two huge restaurants, Zehnder's and Bavarian Inn, which face each other on Main Street. But what many visitors don't realize is that Frankenmuth is home for the state's largest breweries. The oldest is the

G. Heileman Brewing Co. in Frankenmuth

Frankenmuth Brewery, which is located near the corner of Tuscola and Main streets. It began making beer in 1862 as Cass River Brewery and then became Geyer Brewing in 1874. The company was temporarily shut down in 1976 and then reopened the following year under its present name with a German brewmaster arriving to direct the operation. The actual brewery is a state historic site, and plans call for a series of windows to be built so visitors on the outside can watch the beer-making process.

The largest brewery in Michigan, **G. Heileman Brewing Company**, is where Main Street crosses the Cass River. It began as the Frankenmuth Brewery in 1900, producing 10,000 barrels of beer its first year. The brewery survived prohibition by making and selling malt extract for the basement breweries of the local Germans who couldn't understand why their national beverage was now illegal. In 1957 the brewery was bought out by Carling Brewery, which became part of G. Heileman Brewing Company in 1979.

The company (517-652-6161) offers the only brewery tours in the state Monday through Friday at 10 A.M., 11 A.M., 1 P.M., 2 P.M., and 3 P.M. The guided tour begins in the Hospitality Room at the end of the plant, where displays and exhibits explain how beer is made. From there visitors are led through the bottling portion of the brewery to see the beer being poured into bottles, capped, and labeled. The walk ends back at the Hospitality Room, where participants are encouraged to try several of the nine brands of beer and malt liquor the brewery makes. The free tour lasts forty-five minutes.

You can enjoy a stein of the local brew in almost every restaurant and bar in town, but the most intriguing place is **The Tiffany Biergarten** just north of Zehnder's Restaurant on South Main Street. The lumbermen's saloon is located on the first floor of the Hotel Goetz, which was built in 1895 when Frankenmuth was one of the leading logging communities in the Saginaw Valley. The tavern picks up its name from the eighteen Tiffany chandeliers, made in the 1930s. But it is also adorned by a beautiful wooden bar, the original tin ceiling, the inlaid tile floor, and leaded stained glass. Tiffany Biergarten is open from noon until 1 A.M. on Friday and Saturday, when there is live entertainment, and from noon until midnight the rest of the week.

In 1926, the Shriners of Saginaw Valley joined forces with W.S. Butterfield Theaters and broke ground for a building that would serve as a meeting place for the fraternal organization and as a large commercial theater. Less than a year later **The Temple Theatre** opened and was immediately called "the show place of Northeastern Michigan." With a seating capacity of 2,196, it was the largest theater in the state outside Detroit and certainly no less grand than those on Motor City's Woodward Avenue. Its plush carpeting was warm, the red velvet seats rich in appearance, and the domed ceiling, proscenium arch above the stage, and gold walls exquisitely ornate. It also featured a huge crystal chandelier in the lobby and double-width stairways leading up to the balcony. Within the actual theater a Barton organ, purchased in 1927 for $15,000, was installed, while above the stage is the only 70-millimeter screen in mid-Michigan.

The theater was the cultural center for Saginaw from the days of silent films and Vaudeville acts to modern movies. In 1977 it was closed, but several city organizations, intent on saving the historic structure, formed the Temple Theatre Arts Association and reopened the showplace in 1980. Today The Temple Theatre hosts a travelogue series, live concerts and plays, and a popular children's theater series. During the summer it is the site of classic films, and there is no better way to enjoy a classic than on one of the largest screens in Michigan and with original chimes that alert the patrons the intermission is ending. The Temple, located downtown at 203 North Washington Avenue, offers programs year-round. Information on shows and prices is available from the box office (517-752-2471).

Midland County

To most people the city of Midland is Dow Chemical Corporation, the place where Herbert Dow founded his company in 1897 that today gives us everything from Ziploc sandwich bags and Saran Wrap to much of the aspirin used in the country. But Midland is also a city of parks, with 2,700 acres in seventy-four parks scattered throughout the community for a total area that is three times larger than the average area most states allow for parks. The most famous park is Dow Gardens, sixty-six acres of streams, waterfalls, small bridges, and beautifully manicured landscape next to Discovery Square, home of the Midland Center for the Arts.

But the most intriguing is Chippewassee Park, site of the **Tridge**, the only three-way footbridge in the world, city officials proudly claim. The unusual bridge was built in 1981 over the confluence of the Tittabawassee and Chippewa rivers, and its wooden spans connect three different shorelines. In the middle they form a hub where benches overlook the merging currents of two rivers. The Tridge and the nearby riverfront area are the center of activity in downtown Midland. The Midland Music Society hosts free outdoor concerts in the park Thursdays at noon in June and July that have unofficially become known as "Brown Bag-It Days," as office workers will stream down to the area to enjoy their lunch break.

Also located near the Tridge is the Midland Farmer's Market and its 4-H Club petting zoo for children (open Sundays in July from 1 to 4 P.M.) as well as a city-operated canoe livery for a leisurely paddle up the river of your choice. The canoes are rented Saturday and Sunday from 10 A.M. to 7 P.M. in April and May and during the week from 2 to 7 P.M. June through September. The zoo is free, but there is a rental fee for the canoes. In the rest of Chippewassee Park, you'll find a fitness trail, a riverwalk, a picnic area, and an elaborate wooden playscape for children.

Bay County

The shoreline of Saginaw Bay was the final destination for much of the lumber from the valley as thirty-two sawmills were clustered on the waterfront of Bay City. The city flourished on money from timber and shipbuilding, and a drive down Center Avenue shows where much of it went. The lumber barons seemed infatuated with building the most elaborate homes they could afford, and the restored mansions in this historic district overwhelm visitors. In the middle of this Victorian-era street is the Historical Museum of Bay County (517-893-5733), which spins the story of Bay City's golden era through three-dimensional exhibits.

More impressive than the grand homes, however, is the **Bay City City Hall**. Built in 1894, the Romanesque-style stone building dominates the city skyline with its 125-foot clock tower at the southeast corner. It was listed in the National Register of Historic Places, and in 1976 the building underwent major renovation that preserved the original woodwork and distinct metal pillars in the huge lobby. Visitors are welcome to stroll through the massive structure and view the 31-foot Chmielewska Tapestry that hangs in the council chambers. Woven with hand-dyed yarns of 500 colors by a young artist from Poland, the artwork depicts the historic buildings of the community. A climb of sixty-eight steps up the clock tower brings you to a most impressive view of Bay City, the Saginaw River, and the surrounding countryside.

The City Hall (517-894-8147) is located downtown at 301 Washington Avenue and is open from 7 A.M. to 4 P.M. Monday through Friday. Inquire at the Personnel Office at Room 308 for a trip up the clock tower. There is no admission fee.

Many people believe that the sawmills on the Saginaw Bay were replaced by marinas as the area became a recreational paradise for boaters, sailors, and anglers searching its waters for perch, walleye, and bass. From this love of the water evolved **Capt'n Jack's Landing**, a hangout for recreational boaters on the Kawkawlin River north of Bay City. During the summer the restaurant is a lively place with vessels pulling into its docks and landlubbers arriving in the parking lot for its excellent fish and

Bay City City Hall with 125-foot Clock Tower

seafood. The long bar that begins inside curves right through a wall and extends outside onto a huge deck that was built around two trees on the edge of the river. Nothing could be more pleasant on a hot summer day than to be sitting out there at one of the dozen tables, taking in the cool breezes off the bay or the boat traffic motoring slowly through the Kawkawlin. If it's hot, try one of their frozen Nautical House drinks and a heaping plate of cold boiled shrimp.

Arenac County

Iva's in Sterling is not known nearly as well as the Bavarian restaurants in Frankenmuth, nor is it as large an establishment. But the old country roadhouse lacks nothing when it comes to

41

serving a chicken dinner accompanied by bowls of homemade chicken noodle soup, hot biscuits, relish trays, and golden gravy that is ladled on scoops of mashed potatoes and moist dressing. The restaurant dates to 1938 when Iva Ousterhout began renting rooms in her large farm house to the oil-rig workers who were pouring into the tiny town to work in the nearby fields. Iva satisfied the hungry oil men at night with chicken dinners that always began with fresh birds from local poultry farmers.

That has never changed, but the house has. As travelers began hearing of Iva's dinners, the kitchen had to be rebuilt three times to accommodate the extra business, and additional dining areas were added. The house still resembles a roadhouse on the edge of a small farm village, and it still offers Iva's three original styles of chicken: Southern (pan-fried and steamed), American fried (stewed, then fried in an iron skillet), and stewed. Steaks and seafood are also on the menu, but chicken is why travelers stop at Iva's.

From May through October Iva's (517-654-3552) is open daily except Tuesday from 11:30 A.M. until 8:30 P.M. It is closed November and December and open only Thursday through Sunday the rest of the winter. Sterling is 35 miles north of Bay City; to reach the restaurant depart from I-75 at Sterling Road (exit 195) and head east. Dinners range from $5 to $12.

Beginning in Standish is US-23, which follows the Lake Huron shoreline, passing through one small community and city after another until it ends at the Mackinac Bridge. One place that lies hidden off the major route but well worth seeking out is **Point Au Gres Hotel**. The hotel was built in 1939 and has always been a restaurant with an outdoor bar that overlooks Lake Huron at the very tip of the point. Bob Jennings acquired it in 1980 and has been gradually renovating the establishment. In 1987, he reopened the hotel rooms on the second floor. The newly furnished rooms are like a slice of Key West with their ceiling fans, large window views of Lake Huron, and the shared bathrooms down the hall. Overnight guests are treated to a continental breakfast, often served outside on the stone porch along the lake, and use of bicycles and a motor boat. Part of the hotel is the Lamplighter Restaurant, a pleasant spot for dinner with a dozen tables that all face the Great Lake and brick walls that feature waterfowl prints and old wooden decoys. Seafood and steaks are the mainstay of the menu, but if you're lucky the chef will be pan-frying fresh walleye or perch that evening.

To reach Point Au Gres Hotel (517-876-7217) depart south onto Santigo Road (also known as West Street) from US-23 just west of the community of Au Gres. Then head east on Gordon Road for a mile and turn south on Rumsey Road for 1.7 miles. The hotel is at the end of Rumsey Road, and signs point the way from US-23. Rooms range from $27 to $30 per night, while dinners are $8 to $14.

One of Michigan's spring rituals is smelt dipping. You don't need to be a hard-core angler to dip smelt; you just have to possess a love for the small silvery fish that is often deep-fried while wearing a coat of beer batter. The technique is simple: With a bucket roped to your side and a long-handled net you walk into one of the many small streams where the fish spawn. Then in a wide circular motion you swish the net along the bottom of the stream, checking it for smelt after every dip.

Traditionally one of the best spots for smelt dipping is **Singing Bridge**, where US-23 crosses the East Branch of the Au Gres River. So popular is this spot among dippers that the Michigan Department of Natural Resources maintains public access parks on both sides of the bridge. Smelt run late at night during the month of April. Arrive at the bridge at 11 P.M., midnight, or even 2 A.M. during the run and you'll be amazed at the crowd of dippers crammed into the small river. There is usually even a larger crowd on the banks taking in the spectacle. It's hard to tell what night the smelt are going to run, and often dippers depart with little to show for all their work. But when the smelt are running, people leave Singing Bridge with buckets full of one of Michigan's best-loved delicacies.

Across from the bridge is **Singing Bridge Restaurant and Grocery** (517-362-2828), which sells the buckets, nets, and fishing license you need to dip. Or, for those who would just as soon watch and eat but not dip, the restaurant serves delicious smelt dinners during the runs.

Iosco County

Perhaps the most famous river of the logging era was the Au Sable, which begins west of Grayling and ends at Lake Huron between the towns of Oscoda and Au Sable. The river was the chief avenue for bringing out northern Michigan pine, and today much of the land that was cut lies in the Huron National Forest.

The federal forest lies on both sides of the Au Sable and has preserved the logging era at Lumberman's Monument and Visitor's Center which is located 15 miles west of Oscoda along River Road on the banks of the river.

Regulated logging continues, but now the Au Sable is famous among canoers and fly fishermen as a beautiful wooded waterway and the best trout stream east of the Mississippi River. You can drive along the Au Sable for views of it, but a better way is to stop in at **Sawyer Canoe Company**, located on the banks of the river in Oscoda. Although the plant and office are not large, the company is known throughout the country as a manufacturer of fine canoes, especially the sleek and ultra-light racing canoes. The company was started in 1957 by Ralph Sawyer, who wanted a better canoe to compete in the annual Au Sable River Marathon, a 240-mile canoe race from Grayling to Oscoda.

Sawyer went on to build fine racing canoes and win the grueling marathon eight times. The company evolved from the race and today produces dozens of models for racers, recreational paddlers, solo canoeists, and those tackling rough seas. To encourage paddlers to try their canoes, Sawyer runs unguided trips up the Au Sable, by far the best way to see the river. For a fee, Sawyer provides the canoe, paddles, and life jackets as well as transportation to your starting point. You end up back at the Sawyer docks on the Au Sable.

Sawyer Canoes (517-739-9181) will rent either double or solo canoes for a fee that ranges from $19 for a three-hour paddle to $150 for a six-day journey from Grayling to Oscoda. For a weekend trip, it is best to reserve a boat by writing to Sawyer Canoes, 234 South State Street, Oscoda, MI 48750.

Alcona County

At Harrisville, US-23 swings away from Lake Huron and remains inland well into Alpena County. Taking its place along the water in northern Alcona County is Lakeshore Drive, the route to two interesting attractions. The first is **Cedar Brook Trout Farm**, reached 2.5 miles north of Harrisville immediately after turning off US-23. Because of the almost perfect conditions for raising rainbow and brook trout, Cedar Brook was established in the early 1950s as the first licensed trout farm in Michigan. The key to the farm's success is the cold-water springs that flow from the nearby sandy bluffs. The water is funneled into the thirteen ponds and rearing tanks, and its year-round constant temperature (47 degrees) and high level of oxygen are ideal for trout. Its constant flow allows Jerry Kahn, the present owner, to manage without pumps. Kahn begins with eggs and raises the trout from frylings to rainbows that measure well over 16 inches.

The bulk of Kahn's business is shipping thousands of trout in a tank truck to individuals and sportsmen's organizations for stocking their own lakes and rivers. But he also lets travelers stop by and catch their own in two ponds, one stocked with rainbows, the other with brook trout. The water in the ponds is cold and clear, and below the surface you can easily see hundreds of fish swimming around. Throw some feed in the ponds (available from a coin-operated dispenser) and dozens of large fish rise to surface in a feeding frenzy. Anglers are provided with cane poles, tackle, bait, and a warning that catching the trout is not as easy as it looks. No fishing license is needed.

Cedar Brook (517-724-5241), one of the few farms in the state that raises brook trout, is open for fishermen daily from 9 A.M. until 6 P.M. from Memorial Day to Labor Day. The cost per trout depends on the size of fish caught, but for $3 or $4, and a little fishing luck, you can depart with a hefty rainbow.

From the trout farm, Lakeshore Drive continues north and in less than a half mile passes the marked side road to **Sturgeon Point Lifesaving Station** and the preserved lighthouse built in 1869. The last lightkeeper left in 1941, but the U.S. Coast Guard continues to maintain the light. In 1982 the Alcona County Historical Society began renovating the attached lightkeeper's house and soon opened it to the public. The structure is a classic Michigan lighthouse, but the unique feature is that you can climb to the top of the tower (eight-five steps) and not only be greeted by a panorama of Lake Huron but still view a working prism. Amazingly, all that is needed to throw a light miles out on the Great Lake is this huge work of cut glass and an electric light no larger than your smallest finger.

The lightkeeper's house is now a museum with the five rooms downstairs furnished as a turn-of-the-century residence for those who maintained the attached tower. The four rooms upstairs are also open, and each showcases a different aspect of the county's history: shipwrecks, fishermen, the original lightkeepers, and perhaps the most interesting, the ice-collecting industry that boomed

Lighthouse in Alcona County's Lighthouse County Park; lightkeeper's house is a museum

in the area during the winter so iceboxes could be kept cold in the summer.

The lighthouse is operated by a volunteer staff, which tries to keep it open year-round Monday through Thursday from 10 A.M. until 4 P.M. and Saturday and Sunday from noon until 4 P.M. There is no admission, but donations are accepted to maintain it.

Alpena County

Lumbering turned Alpena from a handful of hardy settlers in 1850 into a booming town of 9,000 in 1884, and then when the white pine ran out the community sustained itself by becoming "Cement City," utilizing its huge supply of limestone. From the cement factories emerged Besser Manufacturing Company, the world leader in concrete block-making equipment. Today Alpena is a manufacturing center that can boast the largest population (12,000) and the only enclosed shopping mall in northeast Michigan. But the residents of this modern community also value their past and have begun restoring the historic downtown area as Old Town Alpena.

The original shopping area is clustered around North Second Street and features small and specialized shops that could have been found here as early as the 1920s. One of the most unique stores is **The Country Cupboard**. The antique and general store is located in the old Sepull's Pharmacy, a landmark in Alpena from its opening in 1920 until Hutton Sepull retired in 1986. Outside, its aluminum facing looks plain, but inside it has the character of an old-time pharmacy, which catches unsuspecting visitors by surprise. There are the tin ceiling and the wraparound balcony on the second floor and the traveling ladders that lead up to the ceiling-high shelves, stocked with old medicine containers, apothecary bottles, and boxes of tonic. On the ground floor the walls are lined with hundreds of wooden drawers, each holding some herb, tin of pills, or other merchandise left from pharmacy days.

When the store went on the market Rita and Al Hess couldn't think of a better place to relocate their antique business down the street. They filled the shop with collectibles, baskets, stained glass, and country gifts but kept the old pharmacy atmosphere intact and even began to restore much of the original woodwork. They still sell several of Sepull's more unusual or popular products, including Iceland moss (an herb for folk medicine) and the custom-blended Wellington tobacco.

The Country Cupboard (517-336-6020) is located at 102 North Second Street and is open year-round Monday through Thursday 9:30 A.M. until 5:30 P.M., Friday until 9 P.M., and Saturday until 5 P.M.

Presque Isle County

Jesse Besser, founder of the massive concrete block corporation, was also a humanitarian, and in Alpena the city's noted museum of science, history, and art (the only accredited one in northeast Michigan) is named after him. But Besser was also responsible for leaving something else in Presque Isle County—a small tract of land on Lake Huron whose towering white pines somehow escaped the swinging axes of lumbermen.

The industrial genius, realizing the rarity of the uncut pines and the beauty of undeveloped Lake Huron shoreline, gave the area to the people of Michigan in 1966. Today it is the **Besser Natural Area**, managed by the Department of Natural Resources. The remote preserve, reached by departing US-23 onto County Road 405 to the south end of Grand Lake, offers a small niche of beauty and a little history in a quiet setting. Looping through the Besser Natural Area is a sandy 1-mile-long foot trail, which takes you past a small lagoon that at one time was part of Lake Huron. Look carefully at the bottom of the lagoon (you need polarizing sunglasses on sunny days) and you'll spot the hull of an old ship. The vessel served the community of Bell, which was located here in the 1880s and consisted of 100 residents, several homes, a sawmill, a saloon, a store, and a school.

The most noticeable remains of Bell are the rock pier along Lake Huron, a towering stone chimney, and the collapsed walls of a building whose steel safe and icebox counter indicate it might have been the saloon. Toward the end of the walk you pass through some of the oldest and largest white pines remaining in a state once covered with the trees. There is no fee to enter the preserve, nor is there a visitor's center or any other facility. Descriptive brochures that coincide with the foot path are available from a small box near the trail head.

Visitors who depart from US-23 for the east side of Grand Lake, the state's nineteenth-largest lake with more than 5,000 acres of water, usually want to view lighthouses. They take in the beautifully renovated Old Presque Isle Lighthouse and Museum near the end of County Road 405 (Grand Lake Road) or Lighthouse Park at the very end of the road, where the tallest light tower on the Great Lakes is found standing 109 feet tall. But the **Fireside Inn** is another reason to come to this part of the county, especially for anyone whose idea of a vacation in northern Michigan is renting a quaint log cabin on the edge of a lake. Fireside Inn began its long history as a resort when the original lodge was built in 1908, and the first few authentic log cabins soon began to appear around it. Little has changed about the lodge or the dining room inside with its rustic wooden beams, plank floor, and large windows looking over Grand Lake. They still ring a dinner bell to signal supper time and serve only one entree family style, and afterward guests still wander out to the rambling porch, an immense sitting area 215 feet long, to claim a favorite wicker chair or rocker.

You can rent one of the cabins with a wood interior and stone fireplace or just a room (shared bath) in the lodge itself. Daily rates range from $19 to $50 for the large cabins with three or four bedrooms. Or you can just stop in for dinner, a delightful experience in itself. Dinner prices range from $5 to $7, depending on what is being served that night, and you should call ahead if at all possible. The Fireside Inn (517-595-6369) is located off County Road 405 at the end of the spur, Fireside Highway.

Oscoda County

The state bird of Michigan is the robin, but many argue that it should be the Kirtland's warbler. The small bird, the size of a sparrow with a distinct yellow breast, is an endangered species that breeds only in the jack pines of Michigan. It spends its winters in obscurity in the Bahamas and then migrates to areas between Mio and Grayling, arriving in mid-May and departing by early July. Only in these preserved nesting areas may birders and wildlife watchers have the opportunity to observe this rare bird, of which there are fewer than 200 breeding pairs remaining.

The nesting areas are closed to the public, but you can join a **Kirtland's Warbler Tour**, which is free and sponsored by the U.S. Forest Service office. The tour, which lasts from an hour and a half to two hours, includes a movie and discussion by a forest service naturalist and then a short trip to the nesting area. The guided group hikes through the jack pines, usually covering 1 to 2 miles, until they spot the warblers. Seeing a Kirtland's warbler is not guaranteed, but most tours do see them, especially in late May through June.

This tour is famous among birders who come from all over the country for their only glimpse of the warbler, but it is an interesting stop for anybody intrigued by Michigan's wildlife. The forest service office (517-826-3252), north of Mio on M-33, offers the tour Wednesday, Thursday, and Friday at 7:30 P.M. and Saturday and Sunday at 7:30 A.M. and again at 11 A.M.

Off the Beaten Path in Lake Michigan

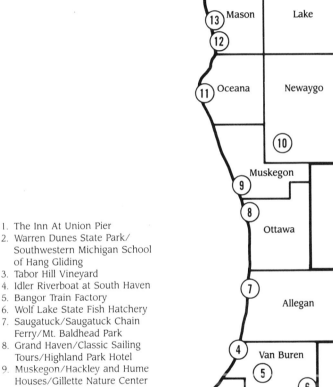

1. The Inn At Union Pier
2. Warren Dunes State Park/
   Southwestern Michigan School
   of Hang Gliding
3. Tabor Hill Vineyard
4. Idler Riverboat at South Haven
5. Bangor Train Factory
6. Wolf Lake State Fish Hatchery
7. Saugatuck/Saugatuck Chain
   Ferry/Mt. Baldhead Park
8. Grand Haven/Classic Sailing
   Tours/Highland Park Hotel
9. Muskegon/Hackley and Hume
   Houses/Gillette Nature Center
10. Gerber Products Company
11. Silver Lake State Park/
    Sandy Korners
12. Bortell's Fisheries
13. White Pine Village in Ludington
14. Nordhouse Dunes
15. Manistee/The Lyman Building
    Museum/Ramsdell Theatre

Lake Michigan

The Lake Michigan shoreline may be the Lower Peninsula's western edge, but many will argue that its heart lies in Chicago. They are now connected by an interstate highway, but that only cemented what was already a long and enduring relationship between the Windy City and this watery edge of Michigan.

It began with the Great Chicago Fire of 1871, which left the city smoldering in ashes. Chicago was rebuilt with Michigan white pine, and the mill towns along the Great Lake, communities like Muskegon and Saugatuck, worked around the clock to supply the lumber. Maybe it was during these excursions to the sawmills that Chicagoans discovered that this region of Michigan possessed more than towering trees and two-by-fours.

They discovered the sand, the surf, and the incredibly beautiful sunsets of the Lake Michigan shoreline. By the 1880s, the tourist boom was on, and it was being fed by vacationers from cities outside Michigan, places like St. Louis, Missouri, and South Bend, Indiana, but most of all from Chicago. They arrived by Great Lake steamships, trains, and eventually automobiles. They caused luxurious resorts and lakeside cottages to mushroom, beginning in New Buffalo on the edge of the Indiana/Michigan border and continuing right up the coast: St. Joseph, South Haven, Saugatuck, Grand Haven, and Muskegon.

They call it the "Michigan Riviera," and even Richard Daley, Chicago's political boss and mayor, had a summer home on the strip. With the completion of I-94 the two regions were linked with a four-lane belt of concrete. Many Chicagoans, eager to escape the heat of their city, were now less than two hours from the cool breezes of their favorite resort.

The Lake Michigan shoreline is still the heart of Michigan tourism. This incredibly beautiful region is characterized by great dunes and watery sunsets, but is also known for its bustling resorts, streets full of quaint shops, and attractive beach-front hotels. The region lies on the western edge of Michigan, but Chicago's influence is unmistakably clear.

Just go to the beach and look at the license plates of the cars, listen to the baseball game the radios are tuned to, or see what city's newspaper someone is snoozing under. You're in Chicago's playland.

Berrien County

You barely cross the state border from Indiana before the first lake-shore communities appear on the horizon with their hotels and motels clustered near the water. Many are new, each with features little different from the one next door. But if you search a little you can find an old inn from another era unique in its appearance and half hidden in a quiet neighborhood near the lake. If you search even harder you might even find **The Inn at Union Pier**.

Union Pier is a cluster of well-shaded streets and nineteenth-century summer homes about 10 miles north of the border. Locate Berrien Street and you'll pass the Inn, three nautical buildings painted light blue with white railings. The Inn began in 1918 as a single building called the Karonsky Resort, but business was so good that by 1929 two more structures were added. An easy journey from Chicago (today it is only ninety minutes by car) the Inn thrived in the golden age of the Lake Michigan resorts but by the 1960s was abandoned and closed up. In 1983, Bill and Madeleine Reinke purchased the place, gutted it, and after two years of renovation, opened for business.

From the outside the most striking feature of the Inn is the wraparound porch on one of the smaller lodges and the matching balcony above it, the place to unwind after a day on the beach. Walkway decks connect the buildings; one has a large hot tub, and tables for breakfast outdoors are on another. Most of the rooms are furnished in light pine and include a Swedish ceramic wood stove. The heart of the main lodge is a spacious common area with a grand piano, overstuffed chairs and sofas, and lots of literature. Guests begin each day with a full breakfast of local fruit and fresh baked goods on the deck and then head across the street to the beach, check out one of the Inn's bicycles, or take to nearby roads for a winery tour or antique excursion.

The Inn at Union Pier (616-469-4700) has fifteen rooms priced for double occupancy from $65 to $85 per night, which includes breakfast. Write ahead for reservations at P.O. Box 222, Union Pier, MI 49129.

The Lake Michigan dunes, the most spectacular natural feature of the region, begin in Indiana and hug the shoreline almost to the Straits of Mackinaw. The largest preserve of dunes in Berrien County is at Warren Dunes State Park, located on the lake 12 miles north of the state border. The park has more than 2 miles of fine sandy beaches and dunes that rise 240 feet above Lake Michigan. The dunes are a popular place during the summer for sunbathers and swimmers during the day and campers at night. But what many don't realize is that Warren Dunes is the only state park that permits hang gliding and is considered by most gliders to be one of the best places in the Midwest, if not the country, for soaring.

Gliders are drawn to the park because of Tower Hill, which looms over the beach parking lot. They trudge up the hill carrying the glider and then soar into the winds from the top, flying over the sandy park or even above Lake Michigan. The sport enjoyed its heyday in the mid-1970s when on a windy weekend there would be almost a hundred gliders on Tower Hill with as many as twenty in the air at one time. The park rangers were so burdened with accidents from unqualified flyers that they instituted a certification system and stricter regulations for gliders.

What makes the park so attractive for these soaring adventurers, especially those just learning the sport, are the smooth winds that come off the lake and the soft and forgiving sand below. Gliding takes place year-round, but the best time is a weekend in the fall or spring with a wind out of the north-northwest. Arrive during those conditions and you'll see a half dozen or so colorful gliders in the air. Or, better yet, sign up for a one-day lesson at **Southwestern Michigan School of Hang Gliding**. Bob Kreske is the owner/instructor, and if the winds are right, at the end of the first day he will have you gliding on a thirty- to forty-second trip. Of course when Kreske flies, he stays up for thirty minutes or more.

The lessons are $80 per person for classes that range from two to four students and include the gliders. Kreske runs his shop (219-778-4974 or 654-7666) out of New Carlisle, Indiana, but all classes meet at Warren Dunes.

Lake Michigan does more than provide water for the beaches or a view from the top of sand dunes. It tempers the winter storms that roll in from the Great Plains and moderates the sweltering summer heat felt elsewhere in the Midwest. These effects, combined with the light soil of the region, have turned the lakeshore strip into a cornucopia of orchards, berry farms, and especially vineyards. Michigan is the third leading wine producing state in the country after California and New York. Paw Paw in Van Buren County is the unofficial center for the state's winemakers, with the largest vineyards, St. Julian Wine Company and Warner Vineyards, located right off I-94.

But smaller wineries are found throughout the region, including a frequent winner in national competition, **Tabor Hill Vineyard and Winecellar**, in the center of Berrien County. The winery began when two Chicago salesmen, who sold steel but loved wine, brought a selection of hybrid grape vines back from France in 1968. They chose their vineyard site in the rolling hills of the county, hoping that the conditions were similar enough to those in France to ensure success.

They were. The transplanted vines thrived, and the winery produced its first bottle in 1970. Seven years later a bottle of its 1974 Baco won a gold medal in the American Wine Competition, and since then both the vineyard and Leonard Olson, the steel salesman turned winemaker, have won numerous awards. The winery remains small, producing 40,000 gallons (or about 15,000 cases) of wine annually in almost two dozen types of whites, reds, and blends.

The best way to view Tabor Hill is on a walking tour that begins where workers bottle the wine and then heads out into the rows of trellised vines in the vineyard for a history of the grapes. You also descend into the wine cellar for a look at the huge vats and hand-carved oak casks that age the wine and then finish the tour in the tasting room for some tips on how to "judge" wine. The twenty-five-minute tour ends with everybody sampling Tabor Hill's finest wines.

The winery also includes an excellent restaurant with tables that overlook the rolling vineyard and a huge deck outside. A favorite activity of many, especially during fall, is to pack a picnic lunch and enjoy it on the open deck with a bottle of Tabor Hill. The winery also holds special events, including its annual Blessing of the Harvest around the first of September, and is the destination for Nordic skiers in the winter, who ski between the rows of vines and along wooded trails. There is a small fee for the cross-country skiing, but it includes a glass of wine at the end to warm up weary skiers.

Tabor Hill (616-422-1161) is on Mount Tabor Road and reached from I-94 at exit 16 by heading north on Red Arrow Highway to Bridgman. From Bridgman head east along Shawnee Road and keep an eye out for the directional signs. This vineyard is definitely off by itself. The free tours are given from 11 A.M. to 5 P.M. Monday through Saturday and noon to 5 P.M. Sunday.

Van Buren County

South Haven has a long and colorful history spiced with Great Lake vessels and shipbuilding, and much of it is explained at the Lake Michigan Maritime Museum, which includes an outdoor boardwalk around several preserved boats. The good life on the lakes can also be enjoyed at dinner time aboard the *Idler* at the **Magnolia Grille**, a restaurant floating in the Black River downtown at Nichols Landing. The *Idler* was built in Clinton, Iowa, in 1897 for Lafayette Lamb, a lumber baron who used the 120-foot houseboat for his own personal use on the Mississippi. They never installed an engine in the *Idler*—Lamb didn't want to be disturbed by the vibrations—so the vessel was always pushed up and down the river by a small tug.

The *Idler* appeared in the 1904 World's Fair in St. Louis, where Vincent Price's father played piano on the boat, but in 1910 it burned to the waterline. It was immediately rebuilt and eventually the boat was purchased and brought to South Haven in 1982. Today it has been beautifully restored, and topside is the Bayou Beach Club, an open-air bar with sweeping views of the town and the Black River from every table. In the Magnolia Grille, located below, you can dine on white-linen in either the original dining quarters or one of four staterooms. Each accommodates a party of six for a private gastronomic evening. The menu lists more than twenty entrees priced from $10 to $16, and every day six new entrees are featured. But many local people know the restaurant best for its Cajun dishes—blackened fish and steak, creoles and gumbos—and its sinfully rich cheesecakes.

Magnolia Grille (616-637-8435) is open daily from 11 A.M. until 10 P.M. Monday through Thursday, until 11 P.M. Friday and Saturday, and on Sunday until 8 P.M. Reservations are accepted and dress is casual on the riverboat.

Not all the attractions of the Lake Michigan region lie near a beach or lake shore. Head inland from South Haven on M-43 and in 12 miles you come to Bangor. A railroad passes through this small town, and there is an old depot situated between the tracks and Railroad Street. Passenger service is still available in Bangor, but that's not why residents describe their home as the "Train City" of Michigan. The depot sat empty for twenty-one years until Lee Miller, a model train enthusiast, chose the building as the site of his Bangor Train Factory. The company produces the Kalamazoo Toy Train and is the only manufacturer in the United States to make Number 1 Grade trains, the largest models, scaled so that a half inch equals a foot.

Tours through the small factory will delight any model train collector or anybody who was deprived of a toy train as a kid. You begin in the showroom where several models are set up and running, and you get a short history of the company and the types of trains it builds. Then you wander into the back to watch workers handcraft each set. Children love the trains, but this is not kid stuff: sets that include 20 feet of track run from $600 to $700.

Tours at the Bangor Train Factory (616-427-7927) are free and offered year-round, but they are especially enchanting during the Christmas season. Hours fall to Christmas are Monday through Saturday 9 A.M. to 4 P.M. and Sunday 1 to 4 P.M. After the holidays, hours are Monday through Friday 10 A.M. to 4 P.M.

Sport fishermen throughout Michigan head for the streams, inland lakes, and Great Lakes to fill their creels with a variety of fish. If they are passing through Van Buren County on M-43, they should also head for the **Wolf Lake State Fish Hatchery**, for this facility is one of the main reasons fishing is so good in Michigan. The hatchery dates back to 1928 and by 1935 was the largest in the world. But construction of the present facility began in 1980, and three years and $7.2 million later the technological upgrading made Wolf Lake the finest complex for producing both warm-water and cold-water species in the country. No other hatchery in Michigan raises as many different species as Wolf Lake, which hatches steelhead, brown trout, chinook salmon, and grayling along with the warm-water species of tiger musky, northern pike, walleye, bass, and bluegill.

Hatchery tours should begin at its new interpretative center, which will fascinate anybody who dabbles in sport fishing. In the lobby there is a wall with plaques of Michigan's record fish—sort of a fishermen's hall of fame—plus displays of the trout fishing on the state's renowned Au Sable River. Off to one side is the "Michigan Room," a walk-through exhibit area that begins with an interesting series of habitat dioramas, cross sections of every type of water you might drop a line into, from trout streams to the Great Lakes. Each diorama shows the species that will be found, the habitat it likes, and the lure of a frustrated angler trying to land the lunkers that lie below. There are also exhibits on fish anatomy, slide presentations of Michigan's commercial fishery, and an area devoted to sport-fishing gear, including a delightful display of more than a hundred different historic lures, plugs, and other tackle. After viewing the exhibits and a short slide presentation in the auditorium, visitors are encouraged to wander through the hatchery itself to view millions of fish in the ponds and rearing tanks.

The center (616-668-3388) is open Wednesday through Friday from 9 A.M. to 4 P.M. and Saturday until 5 P.M. During the summer it is also open Sunday from noon to 5 P.M. and in the winter on Tuesday from 9 A.M. until 4 P.M. There is no admission fee to visit Wolf Lake, which is reached from I-94 by heading north on US-131 for 4 miles and then west on M-43 for 6 miles.

Allegan County

On the map Saugatuck looks like just the next beach-front community along the lake, but in reality it is a trendy resort whose streets are lined with fine restaurants, quaint shops, and lots of tourists. Perhaps the most striking sight in Saugatuck are the docks along the Kalamazoo River, where moored at the edge of the shopping district is an armada of cabin cruisers and sail-boats 30, 40, or 50 feet in length or even longer. You can pick up the boardwalk that winds past the boats on the river anywhere along Water Street, and if you follow it north eventually you'll come to the most unusual vessel afloat, the **Saugatuck Chain Ferry**. It's the only chain-powered ferry in the state, and it has been carrying passengers across the Kalamazoo River since 1838. An operator hand cranks a 380-foot chain attached at each shore, pulling the small white ferry through the water.

It's only 50 cents for the five-minute ride, but it is your escape from the bustling downtown shopping district to one of the most beautiful beaches on the lake. Once on the other side you walk north for a few hundred yards until you reach **Mount Baldhead Park**, with tables, shelter, and a dock on the river. There is also a stairway that takes you (after a little huffing and puffing) to the top of the 200-foot dune where you are greeted with a glorious panorama of Saugatuck, Kalamazoo Lake to the southeast, or Lake Michigan to the west. On the other side you have a choice. You can descend to Oval Beach along the Northwoods Trail, an easy walk that includes a view of the lake and beach along the way. Or you can dash madly down the steep and sandy Beach

The Saugatuck Chain Ferry in Saugatuck

Trail, right off the towering dune, across the beach and into the lake for a cool dip.

Ottawa County

Grand Haven has developed its waterfront along the Grand River and includes a riverwalk that extends several miles from downtown to the picturesque Grand Haven Lighthouse out in Lake Michigan. But by far the most noted aspect of the river is the city's Musical Fountain, the world's largest, which performs nightly during the summer with electronically controlled and synchronized music. Performances begin around dusk (9 to 9:30 P.M.), and most people enjoy the free concerts by assembling in the Waterfront Stadium.

A more unusual way to view the performance is at the end of the sunset cruise offered by the wooden yacht *Francy*, through **Classic Sailing Tours**. The ship, a gaff-rigged skipjack, was built in 1937 and for most of its sealife was used as an oysterboat in the Chesapeake Bay. Chris Veenstra purchased the boat in 1985, brought it back to his hometown of Grand Haven, and restored it. The sailboat departs for three cruises daily, and passengers, who often assist the crew, experience sailing as it was a century ago. By far the most popular trip the company offers is the Sunset Cruise: you first catch the sun melting into Lake Michigan while sipping wine and lounging on the wooden deck and then return to the city to watch the manmade light and music show from the best possible seat in town.

Classic Sailing Tours (616-842-2221) maintains an office in a railroad car behind the old Grand Haven Railroad Depot (now the Tri-City Museum) on Harbor Avenue near the waterfront. Cruises last two and a half hours, and the fares range from $20 to $25.

The Grand Hotel on Mackinac Island has always been famous for its world's longest porch, but at the turn of the century it had a rival in Grand Haven that boasted the "second longest porch in the world." The **Highland Park Hotel** was built in 1889 to become Grand Haven's premier hotel, serving tourists who were mostly from Chicago and St. Louis. It was situated on a bluff overlooking Lake Michigan, and its fifty-one rooms and long porch captured the gentle breezes and sunsets off the lake night after night. It had a superb dining room that hosted such legendary entertainers as Glenn Miller and his band. In 1967, however, the hotel caught fire and burned to the ground, leaving only the most northern section.

Houses now stand where there used to be a hotel, but the portion that was salvaged was purchased by Terry and Judith Postmus in 1985, and now it again offers travelers beach-front accommodations. Judith Postmus also runs an antique store in town, and the six rooms in the hotel reflect her love of restored furnishings. The rooms have their own entrance and a private porch on the second floor where breakfast is served. The hotel also hosts a social hour every evening on one of its two lakefront porches, because—despite the excellent breakfasts and historic atmosphere—its real specialty is sunsets enjoyed most nights along with vintage wines and imported cheeses.

The Highland Hotel (616-842-6483, 846-1473) is open year-round and is right off Harbor Avenue, across from Grand Haven

State Park, at 1414 Lake Avenue. Room rates per night range from $60 to $70, and reservations can be secured by writing the hotel at P.O. Box 346, Grand Haven, MI 49417.

Muskegon County

In the late 1800s, this county was the heart of lumbering on Michigan's western side, and the city of Muskegon grew during the prosperous era to be known as the "Lumber Queen of the World." A drive down West Webster Avenue shows how much money was made and where much of it went: the Victorian mansions are fabulous. But the most elaborate houses were built by the two men who prospered most of all from Michigan white pine, Charles H. Hackley and his partner Thomas Hume. They built their homes next to each other, and it reportedly took 200 artisans and craftsmen two years to complete the houses. Behind the homes the men shared the same carriage house. The **Hackley House** and **Hume House** are listed on the National Register of Historic Places and have been called two of the nation's most outstanding examples of Victorian architecture.

Although restoration continues, the homes are open for tours. The Hackley House is especially impressive, a virtual museum of carved woodwork that strikes you from the moment you walk into the home and are greeted by unusual figures along the walls. Almost every aspect of the house is overwhelming, from its original furnishings and stained-glass windows to the hand-stenciled walls and the eleven fireplaces, each made unique with imported ceramic tiles. If you see only one restored home in Michigan, it should be the Hackley House, where it's hard to imagine living in such style.

The Hackley and Hume Historic Site (616-759-2502) is at 484 West Webster Avenue. Tours are offered May through September, Wednesday, Saturday, and Sunday from 1 to 4 P.M. There is a small admission fee.

The towering dunes along the eastern side of Lake Michigan represent the world's largest accumulation of dunes bordering a body of fresh water and are renowned throughout the country. One of the best places for learning how dunes develop and change is the **Gillette Nature Center** within P.J. Hoffmaster State Park. The center is in fact overshadowed by a huge dune best viewed from the lobby's glass wall to the west. The center features an exhibit hall entitled "The Grain of Sand," which guides you through the natural history of the dunes, and an eighty-two seat theater that uses a nine-projector, multi-image slide show to further explain their delicate nature. On the ground floor there is a gallery that features hands-on exhibits to help children understand the environment of the park.

Most visitors view the exhibits and then hike up to the Dune Platform Overlook. The trail begins next to the center and includes a wooden walkway of 165 steps. It puts you 190 feet above the lake, with spectacular views of the surrounding dune country. There is a vehicle permit fee to enter the state park (616-798-3711), which is reached by heading south of Muskegon on US-31 and exiting at Pontaluna Road and heading west. The Gillette Nature Center is open summer Tuesday through Sunday from 9 A.M. to 6 P.M., during the rest of the year Tuesday through Friday 1 to 5 P.M. and weekends 10 A.M. to 5 P.M.

Newaygo County

Not many tourists go out of their way to see Fremont and nobody stays overnight there—in 1987 the town's only motel was out of business. But an unusual attraction in the farming community of almost 4,000, one that is especially popular with expectant parents, is a tour of **Gerber Products Company**. Fremont is the birthplace of Gerber, the company which in 1928 began manufacturing baby food and forever freed mothers from the tiresome task of straining peas, carrots, and spinach. Fremont continues to serve as the world headquarters for Gerber, which has built a visitor's center in the complex and offers tours Monday through Friday from 9 to 4 P.M.

Tours begin with a short slide presentation in a small auditorium with walls that are filled with Gerber artifacts and memorabilia. Rightfully so, the largest and only color portrait in the room is of Mrs. Daniel F. Gerber, whose idea prompted her husband to turn Gerber from just another canning company into the first manufacturer of baby food. Visitors then board a mini-train for a ride through the processing plant, viewing production lines, packaging, delivery, and the unusual way they make their infant cereal.

The visitor's center (616-928-2614) also includes a gift shop that carries every product Gerber makes, from baby carriages and car seats to clothing and toys—everything except the small jars of strained baby food that the company is best known for. The plant is located at 445 State Street just west of downtown Fremont.

Oceana County

County Road B-15 departs from US-31 north of Whitehall and swings west toward the Lake Michigan shoreline before returning to the highway at Pentwater, the bustling resort community at the northwest corner of Oceana County. Along the way the county road passes Silver Lake, an impressive sight that slows most cars bearing sightseers to a crawl. The lake is bordered to the west by a huge dune that literally towers over it, and from the car window you see beach and sunbathers, crystal clear lake and sailboats, the mountain of sand and dune climbers. Much of what you see, including the strip of dunes that lies between the inland lake and Lake Michigan, is part of **Silver Lake State Park**.

Silver Lake is different from other state parks along Lake Michigan, because the dunes have been divided into three separate areas for three types of users. The region to the south is one of only two places in the state where dune rides are offered in large open-air jeeps that hold up to twelve passengers (Mac Wood's Dune Rides, 616-873-2817). The section in the middle is the pedestrian area, where people scramble up the huge dunes and hike across them to Lake Michigan.

But it is the northern area of the park that is most unique, as it is designated for off-road vehicles. This is the ORV capital of the Midwest, the only public dunes in Michigan where people can drive their three- and four-wheelers, dirt bikes, trail jeeps, or any other vehicle built for the soft sand and steep terrain. On almost any day of the summer the ORV parking lot at the end of Hazel Road will be filled with a wide assortment of vehicles, their drivers, and the trailers and vans they arrived in. They come from Indiana, Illinois, Ohio, and Wisconsin to ride here, as well as from all over Michigan. Pedestrians don't venture into the motorized area, but there is a wooden viewing platform overlooking the ORV entry point. Here you can view all the daredevil drivers and their machines as they climb the first dune.

For the more adventurous, **Sandy Korners** offers guided drives on the dunes. Each person is given a four-wheel all-terrain vehicle, helmet, and instructions on safe usage. A guide then leads the group for a one- to two-hour run across the sandy hills. Sandy Korners (616-873-5048) is on Hazel Road before you enter the state park and charges $25 an hour for the rides. All participants must have a driver's license. There is a vehicle fee to enter Silver Lake State Park (616-873-3083).

Mason County

Continue on South Lakeshore Drive, pass the huge Ludington Power Plant, and then after a few miles keep an eye on the east side of the road for **Bortell's Fisheries**. From the outside the fish market is not glamorous, but it has been in business since 1937 and gradually has evolved into west Michigan's finest shop for fish and seafood. They carry a variety of frozen seafood, make delicious marinated herring in cream and wine, and smoke one of the best selections of fish in the state, including trout, chub, salmon, sturgeon, blind robin, and menominee. Want something fresher? When in season their cases are filled with fresh perch, pike, walleye, trout, and even smelt in the spring, all half buried in ice.

Still not fresh enough? Then you can wander around back with a pole and catch a rainbow trout out of one of their stocked ponds. They will cook any fresh fish right there in the market and serve it with French fries and homemade potato salad or coleslaw. You can enjoy your meal outside at one of half a dozen picnic tables next to the market or better yet cross the street to Summit Park where you have a view of Lake Michigan from your table. The freshest fish, good food, and beautiful scenery at a little out-the-way county park—it doesn't get much better than that.

Bortell's Fisheries (616-843-3337) is 7 miles south of Ludington on South Lakeshore Drive between Meisenhiemer and Deren Roads. From May through September the store is open daily from 11 A.M. until 8 P.M.

The first frame house in Mason County was built by Aaron Burr Caswell in 1849. Six years later the two-story home was still the only frame building in an area that was trying to organize itself into Michigan's newest county. So that year Caswell offered the front half of his home as the first courthouse and county seat of Mason. Today the preserved building is a state historic site and the centerpiece of **White Pine Village**, a museum complex operated by the Mason County Historical Society.

Trapper's cabin in White Pine Village in Ludington

The village is composed of some twenty preserved buildings or replicas, all from the surrounding county and set up along streets on a bluff overlooking Lake Michigan. Each of the buildings, which range from an 1840s trapper's log cabin to a hardware store of the early 1900s, is completely renovated inside and is viewed on a leisurely self-guided walk. Throughout the village people in traditional dress apply their trades, everything from a blacksmith to a turn-of-the-century housewife cooking on a wood stove to a violin maker.

What makes White Pine Village an enjoyable experience is the active visitor participation in the exhibits. A documented trial that was held in the Caswell home in the 1860s is re-enacted today with visitors filling in as the jury and nine out of ten times handing down the same verdict as the first time. A log chapel on the

65

rise overlooking the area still holds Sunday service, and afterward people are encouraged to help the village cooks and enjoy their fresh baked treats.

White Pine Village (616-843-4808) is open from Memorial Day until Labor Day daily from 11 A.M. until 5 P.M. but hosts a variety of special events including musical programs every Tuesday at 7 P.M. The museum complex is located off US-31, 3 miles south of Ludington, and is reached by exiting west onto Iris Road and then turning north at South Lakeshore Drive for a quarter of a mile. There is a small admission fee.

From Ludington the famous dunes of Lake Michigan continue to the north, and the area immediately adjacent to the city has been preserved as the Ludington State Park. It's a popular place where visitors enjoy miles of beach, rolling dunes, modern campgrounds, or the hike to historic Point Sable Lighthouse. Where Ludington State Park ends, the **Nordhouse Dunes** begin, a 1,900-acre preserve in the Manistee National Forest that is not as well known or visited as much as the state park but equally beautiful.

A Michigan governor called the Nordhouse Dunes "one of the most outstanding scenic resources" in the state, and they are presently being considered for federal wilderness designation. What makes these dunes so unique is that the area is entirely undeveloped. Travel through the dunes is only on foot along either 10 miles of easy-to-follow trails or by simply making your way across the open hills of sand. The area is the only place in Michigan where you can hike in and camp among the dunes. Because of its inaccessibility to motorized traffic, the dunes area also offers the opportunity, for those willing to hike in, of having a beach to themselves along its 4 miles of sandy lake shore.

Access into Nordhouse Dunes is through the Lake Michigan Recreation Area, a semiprimitive campground on the northern end of the preserve that is maintained by the Manistee Ranger District (616-723-2211) of the national forest. Trails into the dunes begin from the recreation area, which also contains one hundred camping sites, a beach, and observation towers overlooking the lake. To reach the recreational area take US-31 to Lake Michigan Road (also known as Forest Road 5629) located 10 miles south of Manistee. Follow Lake Michigan Road 8 miles west to the area. There is no fee for exploring the dunes or day use of the recreational area. There is a nightly fee for camping.

Manistee County

Manistee is another lake-shore town that boomed during the lumbering era and at one time in the late 1800s boasted thirty-two sawmills and seventeen millionaire lumber barons among its residents. Almost the entire town was destroyed in the Great Fire of 1871 on the very day Chicago experienced one of its worse blazes. One of the first buildings erected after the fiery mishap was the Lyman Building, which was a place of business throughout its existence until the Manistee County Historical Society turned it into the only "storefront museum in the state."

The Lyman Building Museum is not just another county museum displaying local artifacts. The many fixtures, walk-in vault, and wraparound balcony have been preserved, and part of the first floor has been restored as an early drug store with brass apothecary scales, pill makers, an impressive selection of antique medicines and balms, and fading posters on the walls selling Pe-Ru-Na, which "cures catarrh." The other half of the first floor is set up as a general store, while in the back is an old newspaper office with original Linotype machines.

Upstairs there are ten more rooms, including a dentist's office, a bank, and the living room of an early 1900s home. The hallway between the rooms is filled with Victor talking machines and Victrolas. The Lyman Building (616-723-5531), at 425 River Street in downtown Manistee, is open year-round and daily from May to November from 10 A.M. until 5 P.M., Monday through Saturday from June 1 to October 1, and Tuesday through Saturday the rest of the year. There is no admission fee.

Another impressive building left over from the town's golden lumbering era is the **Ramsdell Theatre**, built in 1903 by Thomas Jefferson Ramsdell and today listed on the National Register of Historic Places. Ramsdell, a local lawyer and later a state legislator, wanted to add some culture to the rough-and-tumble logging town and built one of the most elaborate opera houses in the state. It featured a double balcony upstairs and private viewing boxes along the main floor. It was proclaimed "acoustically perfect," and famed theatrical artist Walter Burridge painted the main curtain, which is still used today. Other paintings adorn the dome and archways of the lobby.

Citizens saved the theater from demolition in the 1920s, and the city finally purchased the structure in 1943. Today the Manistee Civic Players operate the facility and use it to stage a summer series of plays. Stop in when the box office is open (a week before each show, Monday through Saturday from noon to 6 P.M.) and you can view the interior. Or call (616-723-9948) for a tour of the opera house. Ramsdell Theatre is on First and Maple streets.

Off the Beaten Path in Northwest Michigan

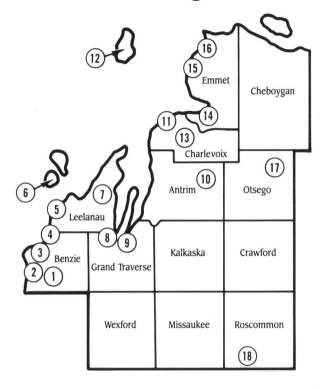

1. Gwen Frostic Prints
2. Northwest Soaring Club of Frankfort
3. Chimney Corners Lodge
4. Platte River Point
5. Sleeping Bear Point Coast Guard Station Maritime Museum
6. South Manitou Island
7. Boskedel Vineyard
8. Malabar Bed and Breakfast in Traverse City
9. Adventures Beyond Balloon Tours
10. Deadman's Hill
11. Fishermen's Island State Park
12. Beaver Island
13. Horton Bay General Store
14. Little Traverse Historical Museum
15. Legs Inn
16. Bliss Township Park
17. Pigeon River Country State Forest
18. North Higgins State Park/Civilian Conservation Corps Museum

Northwest Michigan

In many ways, Northwest Michigan is a continuation of the region stretching along Lake Michigan. It's accented by vast tracts of dunes, miles of beaches, and a handful of well-developed resort towns whose specialty shops bustle in the summer and winter. But it is also distinctly different.

This is "the land of many little bays," with scenic Grand Traverse Bay dominating the center of the region, Little Traverse Bay farther up the shoreline, and remote Sturgeon Bay at its northern tip. For many tourists this is Mackinaw City, a tour of Fort Michilimackinac, and a ferry ride to Mackinac Island, the summer resort island known throughout the country for its horse-and-carriage transportation and the Grand Hotel.

But most of all, this is Michigan's Cherry Country. Moderate weather from the Great Lakes and light soils help this region produce 80 to 85 percent of the state's total cherry crop. Drive along US-31 from Traverse City to Charlevoix in spring and you'll pass rolling hills of trees in full bloom and air scented by cherry blossoms.

Arrive in July and you can enjoy the bountiful harvest these fruit farms produce. Along this 50-mile stretch of road you'll pass dozens of farms and will undoubtedly see harvesting crews "shaking" one tree after another, with the cherries ending up in a large metal tank of water.

You'll also see numerous roadside fruit stands that will be hard to pass up, and you shouldn't even try. The most common sweet cherries sold are Bing and Schmidt; tourists often call them black cherries though if they are, the fruit is overripe. Look for cherries that are firm and dark maroon in color, and be prepared when you bite into your first one. The juice will explode from the cherry, dribble down your chin, and send your taste buds into a state of ecstasy. There are few things as wonderful in this state as a northern Michigan cherry in July.

Benzie County

One of the smallest counties in the state, Benzie is also one of the most scenic. It features rolling forested hills, spring-fed trout streams, towering sandy bluffs, and endless beaches along Lake Michigan and Crystal Lake, a body of water whose clarity lives up to its name. In the natural beauty of this northwoods setting, Gwen Frostic emerged as one of Michigan's most noted poets and publishers from her background as an artist and a conservationist. Her love of nature has always been with her, but she began writing and carving blocks for prints in the mid-1940s in the blue-collar community of Wyandotte, located south of Detroit. In the early 1960s she moved to a wooded spot 2 miles west of Benzonia and set up **Gwen Frostic Prints** on a personal wildlife sanctuary of 285 acres.

Her large gallery is housed in a building of native stone, glass, and old wood, which seeks to "bring the outdoors in" while blending into the natural surroundings. She accomplished that surprisingly well. Inside you'll walk below rough-cut beams past huge stone fireplaces, and view the tumbling water of natural fountains. You'll be surrounded by Frostic's woodblock prints, tables covered with books of her poetry, and bird carvings by some of the country's leading wildlife carvers. There is a small library overlooking a pond where waterfowl usually are feeding, and another room displays all the honors she has received, including the proclamation of an official "Gwen Frostic Day" set aside by a Michigan governor.

Most impressive, perhaps, is the publishing aspect of the gallery. From a balcony above, visitors can view fifteen original Heidelberg presses clanking away as workers print a wide selection of cards, notepaper, wall prints, and books, all using block designs carved by Frostic, featuring natural subjects and sold in the gallery. The artist/poet is now in her eighties and lives on the top floor of the gallery, but she regularly comes down to meet her patrons and autograph copies of her books.

Gwen Frostic Prints (616-882-5505) is at 5140 River Road, 2 miles west of US-31 and 6 miles east of M-22 in Frankfort. The gallery is open daily from May to November from 9 A.M. until 5:30 P.M. and until 4:30 P.M. Monday through Friday the rest of the year. The presses are in operation only Monday through Friday.

Back in the 1930s, a small group of Frankfort residents discovered the thrill of soaring in gliders. They would take off from the high bluffs overlooking Lake Michigan and soar through the air, sometimes for hours, before landing on the beach. What emerged was the **Northwest Soaring Club of Frankfort**, which at one time hosted a national soaring championship in this small town.

The art of soaring has changed over the years, but the club is still around, offering lessons and, for visitors passing through on vacation, introductory rides. Passengers join a certified pilot in a two-seat glider that measures 25 to 35 feet in length, with a wingspan of around 50 feet. The glider is towed 2,000 to 3,000 feet in the air by a small plane and then released. What follows is a spectacular, and quiet, ride along the Lake Michigan shoreline with immense views of the lake, sand dunes, and beautiful Crystal Lake. The length of the ride depends on the wind and thermal conditions of the day, but it ranges from thirty minutes to sometimes several hours.

Introductory rides are offered from May through October and cost $25 per person. Interested persons should call ahead by contacting either Rudi Trunk (616-946-1533), Hal Bruning (616-882-5147), or John House (616-352-7340). The club now takes off from Frankfort Airport located on Airport Road, south of M-115.

The Northwoods Inn, a rural lodge built of hand-stripped logs, is located on the northern shoreline of Crystal Lake. In the glow of a huge stone fireplace, one may be served dinner once or even twice an evening. **Chimney Corners** is actually a resort that for the past fifty years has been renting out cabins and cottages. But its main lodge is a 1910 cabin built on a wooded hillside and filled with antiques, throw rugs, and a main dining room with only seven tables but nice views of the lake below. Its kitchen is filled with cast-iron skillets and pots and some very skillful cooks. Mollie Rogers directs the kitchen staff and treats her patrons to only one entree each evening—but when that entree is a dish such as Cornish game hens, rosemary-stuffed leg of lamb, or duck a l'orange, there is no need for choices.

Chimney Corners (616-352-7522) is on M-22, 7 miles north of Frankfort, and its dining room is open to the public. Dinner, which ranges in price from $10 to $13, is a single seating Monday through Wednesday at 6:30 P.M. On Thursday through Saturday it is served at 6 P.M. and again at 7:30 P.M. They can seat only fifty people at the old lodge, so reservations are strongly recommended.

Of all the dunes along Lake Michigan, the best known within the state and around the country are those in Sleeping Bear National Lakeshore, administered by the National Park Service. Thousands visit the area every year, and many head straight to the "Dune Climb," a 150-foot steep hill of sand located right off M-109 in Leelanau County. This is the park's most famous feature, a knee-bending climb up the towering dune and a wild run down through the soft sand. But there are other aspects of the park, many having nothing to do with dunes and often overlooked by visitors who rush through the area in an afternoon.

The national lake shore begins in Benzie County and includes one of most scenic beaches on Lake Michigan. **Platte River Point** is a long, sandy spit divided from the mainland by the crystal clear Platte River. It's pure sand, this narrow strip, with endless Lake Michigan on one side, the knee-deep salmon and trout river on the other, and panoramas of towering dunes off in the distance. To reach it, sunbathers turn west from M-22 onto the marked Lake Michigan Road and follow it to its end. Then it's a quick wade through the rippling waters of the Platte River with dad holding young ones or the picnic lunch high on his shoulder. There is no bridge.

People at Platte River Point swim, build sand castles, and beachcomb as on any other beach. But the favorite activity here is floating. They bring out an old inner tube or an air mattress, hike a few hundred yards up the point, and then allow the Platte River to give them a free ride right out to Lake Michigan if they wish. It's debatable who enjoys it more, the kids or the parents. If you don't have an inner tube, you can rent one from Casey's Corner (616-325-3636) located on M-22 right before you turn off for the beach. They rent tubes for one to four persons and even have dropoff and pickup services for those who want to spend an afternoon "tubing" the Platte River from the Platte Lake to the Great Lake. Rental rates vary depending on the length of your float and the size of the tube.

Leelanau County

Today Sleeping Bear National Lakeshore is known for its spectacular dune terrain, best viewed along the Pierce Stocking Scenic Drive. At the turn of the century, however, the noted feature of this area was the Manitou Passage, which lies between the Manitou Islands and the mainland. During the heyday of Great Lake shipping from the 1860s to 1920, when on a single day a hundred vessels might pass through, this was a shoal-lined short cut they all followed. Manitou Passage's shallow reef-like shoals, narrow passage, and often violent weather produce more than its share of shipwrecks, and eventually several lighthouses and lifesaving stations were built on the mainland and the islands.

One of them has been preserved by the National Park Service as **Sleeping Bear Point Coast Guard Station Maritime Museum**. The facility began its service in 1901 as a U.S. Life Saving Station and was actually situated on Sleeping Bear Point. But in 1930, with a migrating sand dune threatening to bury it, the U.S. Coast Guard (having replaced U.S. Life Saving Service) moved the buildings 1.5 miles toward Glen Haven. The station ended its duty in 1942 and now is a well-restored museum that tells the story of the U.S. Life Saving Service, which manned the coastline all around the country.

Anywhere from six to ten men would live at the remote station, and their former living quarters, a huge two-story building, is now the main exhibit area. It allows visitors a glimpse of the regimented work they performed and the isolated life they lived. Nearby the boathouse contains the life-saving boats, complete with tracks down to the beach for quick launching, and other equipment, including the beachcart. When ships ran aground within 400 yards of shore the life savers would pull out the beachcart and use the small cannon on it to shoot a guide line onto the distressed vessel. That rope was used to string more lines across the water, and a "breeches buoy" was sent to the ship on a pulley. Then one by one sailors would step into the breeches of the buoy and ride the line to the shore and safety.

Check with the park headquarters (616-326-5134) in Empire for time and day of the museum's "Heroes of the Storm" program, when rangers demonstrate a turn-of-the-century shipwreck rescue using the beachcart, the breeches buoy, and volunteers from the audience who fill in for sailors and life savers. Only the cannon is missing.

The village of Leland's trademark is a row of weathered dockside shacks along the Leland River that at one time housed commercial fishermen and today is a historic district known as Fishtown. All the commercial fishermen except Carlson Fisheries have disappeared from the strip, but their buildings have been preserved and now house specialty shops and stores. With its unique setting and atmosphere, Fishtown is the proper place to begin a nautical adventure to **South Manitou Island**, the portion of the Sleeping Bear National Lakeshore located 17 miles from Leland in Lake Michigan.

Island visitors board a ferry at the end of Fishtown and begin with a ninety-minute cruise to South Manitou that passes a lighthouse and the scenic shoreline of Sleeping Bear Dunes. The island, with its hardwood forests and natural harbor, attracted settlers, a lighthouse, and a life saving station as early as 1840, and it possesses an interesting history. The ferry has a four-hour layover at the national park dock, more than enough time to view the small museum at the visitor's center, climb the 116 steps to the top of the lighthouse, and enjoy a lunch on the nearby beaches.

For the more energetic, there are trails and old farm roads across the island, and it's possible to hike the 6-mile round trip to the *Francisco Morazan* and return to the mainland the same day. The *Morazan* was a Liberian freighter that ran aground in November, 1960, in the southwest corner of the island, and a large portion of the battered vessel is still visible above the waterline today. But for the best adventure on South Manitou, camp for a night or two at Weather Station Campground, a national park facility that is free. The campground is a 1.5-mile hike in from the dock, and you can explore the tract of sand dunes on the west side of the island. The dunes, perched high above Lake Michigan on bluffs, are probably the most remote and least visited ones in Michigan.

All visitors must bring their own food to South Manitou, and campers have to be self-sufficient with tent, sleeping bags, and other equipment. Contact Manitou Island Transit (616-256-9061 or 271-4217) regarding the ferry that sails for the island daily June through August. Round-trip fares range from $8 to $14.

The growing conditions in southwest Michigan that made Paw Paw the wine-producing center of the state are also found in Leelanau and Old Missionary, two peninsulas filled with fruit farms and a half dozen vineyards of surprising quality. All the vineyards have a tasting room, and an interesting day can be had visiting each one of them. But the first bonded wine cellar in the area—and many think the most beautiful one in the state—is **Boskydel Vineyard**, a small winery on the shores of Lake Leelanau. There is no restaurant at Boskydel or even any picnic tables outside, but it is built on the side of a hill and from the parking lot you have a view of the sloping vineyard leading down to the huge lake, framed by the rolling hills of the Leelanau Peninsula. All this prompted one wine critic to proclaim Boskydel the most beautiful site for a winery in the country.

It was within the family tradition that Bernie Rinke should plant a vineyard. He grew up on an Ohio farm, and his father bootlegged wine during Prohibition. Rinke began planting his vineyard in 1964 and now cultivates twenty-five acres of grapes, producing 6,000 gallons (2,500 cases) annually of several dry and semi-dry red and white table wines. The tasting room is open daily year-round from 1 to 6 P.M., and if you want a tour of the winery, Rinke will lead you through a ten-minute look of his facility.

But Rinke would rather stay in the small tasting room, plop a large wine glass in front of you (no plastic cups here), and talk ... about his grapes, about wine tasting, about his days as Northwestern Michigan College's first librarian in nearby Traverse City (ask him where the name of the winery comes from). A beautiful vineyard, a most delightful winemaker, and not a bad wine either. Boskydel (616-256-7272) is 3.5 miles southeast of the town of Lake Leelanau on the corner of County Road 641 and Otto Road.

Grand Traverse County

The most noted feature of the county is Grand Traverse Bay, a beautiful body of water that is outlined by Traverse City to the south and split up the middle by Old Missionary Peninsula. Its protected waters have become a haven for sailboats, catamarans, and wind surfers, but by far the most impressive vessel afloat during the summer is the *Malabar*, an 1850 replica of a two-masted, gaff-rigged, topsail schooner. The 105-foot, 100-ton ship was built in 1975 in Bath, Maine, and splits its sailing days with summers in Traverse City and winters in Key West.

It is built to look and sail like a traditional schooner, and it's that love for old wooden sailboats that draws most of its passengers on deck. From May to mid-October the *Malabar* offers three sailings daily, with two-hour cruises at noon and 3 P.M. and a three-hour sunset sail—the most popular trip of course—at 6:30 P.M. But those passengers who romance about a life on the high seas go a step further and book a cabin on the *Malabar*, which at

Malabar: floating bed and breakfast in Traverse City

night becomes Michigan's only floating bed and breakfast. The quarters are tiny, with bunks built into the curves and angles of the hull. The head is shared, and the showers are back on land. But in the evening guests wander topside to take in Traverse City lights shimmering on the bay or snuggle up in their bunks to be put to sleep by the gentle swells and the creaking of a wooden hull.

The *Malabar* is operated by Traverse Tall Ship Co. (616-941-2000). Its office and dock are at 13390 West Bay Shore Drive. Daily cruises range from $18 to $23 for adults, and overnight accommodations, which include a hearty breakfast with the crew in the galley, are $35 to $60 for singles or doubles.

You can also enjoy the water from above through **Adventures Beyond Balloon Tours**, which offers hot-air balloon tours across Grand Traverse Bay, often beginning in the Chateau Grand Traverse vineyards on Old Missionary Peninsula. This may well be the most spectacular view from any hot-air balloon in Michigan, as below you lies the narrow peninsula, the rippling waters of the bay, Traverse City, or the endless rows of the cherry orchards to the northeast. The entire flight takes three hours, with an hour in the air, and flights are always held at sunrise or sunset (less wind turbulence). They are priced at $135 per person, but available Monday through Friday are shorter morning flights of fifteen to thirty minutes that range in price from $40 to $75 per person. Jeff Geiger, the Traverse City balloonist who runs Adventures Beyond (616-943-9386), recommends reservations but says he can usually fulfill last-minute urges to float above the bay.

Antrim County

Speeding along US-131 in the middle of Antrim County, you pass one of the most spectacular inland viewing points in the Lower Peninsula, though you would never know it from this road. The side road to **Deadman's Hill** is 7 miles north of Mancelona, but there is little fanfare about the scenic overlook: Only a small, brown sign points the way. Follow Deadman's Hill Road for 1.5 miles until it dead-ends at a pair of Department of Natural Resources pit toilets and a wood-chip path. Some 15 yards up the path is a spectacular panorama from the high point of over 1,200 feet. You take in a 180-degree view of the Jordan River valley stretching 15 miles to rugged hills that fill the horizon. During October the view from this spot is priceless, as the entire valley with the winding river through it is on fire with autumn reds and oranges.

Deadman's Hill reaches a high point of 1,257 feet and earned its name from the logging era at the turn of the century. The steep hills made the Jordan River valley a treacherous place to log, and numerous accidents occurred. But they grieved the most in 1910 when "Big Sam" Graczyk, twenty-one years old and soon to be married, was killed while driving a team of horses and a big wheel of logs. The name for the ridge stuck. You can admire the view, have a picnic while sitting on the edge, or the more adventurous can hike the Jordan River Pathway which begins at this point. Part of the trail is a 3-mile loop down to the river and back, or it can be turned into an 18-mile overnight walk to a hike-in campground for backpackers.

Charlevoix County

South of Charlevoix off of US-31 is yet another state park along Lake Michigan. **Fisherman's Island State Park** possesses many of the same features as the other parks: 3 miles of sandy shoreline, excellent swimming areas, some scenic views of the Great Lake. But Fisherman's Island also has a couple of unique features. Not nearly as popular or crowded, the park offers fifteen rustic campsites right on Lake Michigan. Each one is tucked away in the trees with a table and a spot to pitch a tent only a few feet from the lapping waters of the lake. These are some of the most beautiful campsites in the Lower Peninsula, and naturally they are the first to be chosen in the campground. Be prepared to camp on an inland site the first night and then claim a lakeside one first thing the next morning.

The other noted feature of the state park is the Petoskey stones. The state stone is actually petrified coral, a leftover fragment of the many coral reefs that existed in the warm-water seas from Charlevoix to Alpena some 300 million years ago. Today the stone is collected by rock hounds, and many of them end up polished and used in jewelry, paperweights, and other decorative items. Dry stones are silvery with no apparent markings to the untrained eye, but when the rocks are wet it's easy to see the ringlike pattern that covers them. Rock hounds searching for the stones are usually seen closely inspecting the waterline or washing off handfuls of rocks in the lake.

The 2.5-mile park road begins at the ranger station and ends at the sandy beaches of the state park but along the way passes an extended rocky shoreline. Many gem enthusiasts say this is one of the best places in northern Michigan to find Petoskey stones. Stop at the ranger station for a park map and hand-out on the famous stone. There is a vehicle fee to enter Fisherman's Island State Park (616-547-6641) and an additional charge of $4 to camp overnight.

The Great Lakes that have blessed Michigan with miles of magnificent shoreline also have given it many islands that have become unique destinations for visitors. The most popular is Mackinac Island, the non-motorized resort (no cars or buses) that tourists flock to each summer, taking ferries out of Mackinaw City in the Lower Peninsula or Saint Ignace across the Mackinac Bridge on the Upper Peninsula. But there are many other islands without the crowds, commercialization, and fudge shops of Mackinac that make for an interesting side trip. One of the largest is **Beaver Island**, reached by a ferry from Charlevoix.

Known as "Emerald Isle" for its strong Irish heritage, Beaver Island lies 32 miles northwest of Charlevoix and is 55 square miles of forests, inland lakes, and farms. Its recorded history dates back to 1832, when Bishop Frederic Baraga, the Snowshoe Priest, brought Christianity to a small Indian settlement there. But the island's most bizarre period began in 1847 after James Jesse Strang arrived. Strang and his band of Mormon followers had just broken away from the leadership of Brigham Young and established St. James, the island's only village. Eventually Strang would crown himself "King of Beaver Island" and rule the island and its religious sect with an iron hand before being shot in 1856 by a disgruntled subject. Irish immigrants followed in the 1870s to fish the waters of northern Lake Michigan, and today many of the 350 people who live year-round in or near St. James have roots back in Ireland.

Beaver Island has an assortment of lodge and hotel accommodations and restaurants for overnight visitors, but on Saturdays in July and August it also makes an ideal day trip. You can depart from Charlevoix at 8:30 A.M. on the ferry and reach the island by 11 A.M. for a six-hour visit before catching the last ferry back to the mainland at 5:30 P.M. In St. James there are two museums: the

Old Mormon Print Shop, which was built by King Strang in 1850, and the Marine and Harbor Museum, a 1906 net shed dedicated to the time when the area bustled with fishermen.

You can also rent a moped and tour the island, which has more than a hundred miles of roads, most of them dirt and gravel. On a pleasant summer day this is a most delightful adventure and a great way to see the old farmhouses, inland lakes, remote shoreline, and lighthouse located outside of St. James. Pack a picnic lunch and plan on motoring three to four hours to circle Beaver Island. Beaver Island Boat Co. (616-547-2311) runs the ferry and charges $17 for a round-trip adult ticket. Beaver Island Sports and Rental (616-448-2266) in St. James rents mopeds or cars at $6 an hour or $40 a day. For a complete list of island businesses, lodging, and sites contact Beaver Island Civic Association, P.O. Box 5, Beaver Island, St. James, MI 49782, (616-448-2505).

A number of writers have ties to Northwest Michigan but none as famous as Ernest Hemingway, who spent the summers of his youth at his family's cottage on Walloon Lake. Hemingway buffs often tour the area to view artifacts and places that made their way into his writing. Most begin in Petroskey's Little Traverse Bay Historical Museum (see Emmet County) and then head down US-131 past Walloon Lake. Some go to Hemingway Point on the south shore of Lake Charlevoix, where the young author once fled (it was owned by his uncle) when being pursued by a game warden. But almost all eventually stop at the **Horton Bay General Store**, located across the lake on Boyne City Road.

Built in 1876 with a high false front, the store's most prominent feature is its large front porch with benches and stairs at either end. Hemingway idled away some youthful summers on that porch and fished nearby Horton Creek for rainbow and brook trout. He also celebrated his first marriage in Horton Bay's Congregational Church and eventually the general store appeared in the opening of his short story "Up in Michigan." The Horton Bay General Store has had a string of owners, but remarkably little has changed about its appearance. It is still the classic general store; only the bright red benches outside receive a new coat of paint every now and then.

You enter through a flimsy screen door with a bell above it and inside you find the worn wooden floors and shelves stacked with canned goods and other merchandise. There is an old wooden tub filled with ice and cold drinks, a small freezer that holds four or five flavors of ice cream, and the lunch counter where the morning coffee drinkers gather. Then as your eyes wander toward the ceiling you realize this is more a preserved shrine to Hemingway than a store for the local residents. On one wall hang guns, old traps, mounted deer heads, and a panel of photographs of the author during his days in Northwest Michigan. Horton Bay General Store is open from 9 A.M. until 10 P.M. Monday through Friday and from 9 A.M. until 5 P.M. on Sunday.

Emmet County

Housed in Petoskey's Chicago and West Michigan railroad depot, which was built in 1892, the **Little Traverse Historical Museum** is the first logical stop of any Hemingway tour. The display case is small but contains photographs, other memorabilia, and some rare first edition books that Hemingway autographed for his friend Edwin Pailthrorp, whom he visited in Petoskey in 1947. There is also a display case devoted to another famous writer, Bruce Catton, who was born in the Emmet County town and grew up in nearby Benzonia. Later Catton would pen *A Stillness at Appomattox*, for which he won a Pulitzer Prize in 1953. The original manuscript of that book and other personal artifacts now are in the museum.

The museum (616-347-2620) is on Dock Street on Petoskey's picturesque waterfront and is open April through October from 9 A.M. until 4:30 P.M. Monday through Saturday. There is no admission fee.

From the well-developed resort town of Harbor Springs, M-119 departs north and hugs the coastline for 31 miles until it ends at Cross Village. It is often cited as a scenic drive, but not for the views of Lake Michigan you might expect when tracing it on a map. This is the "Tunnel of Trees" Shore Drive, a narrow road that climbs, drops, and curves its way through the thick forests along the rugged coast. At times the branches from trees at each side of the road merge overhead to indeed form a complete tunnel, shading travelers even when the sun is beaming down at midday. You finally emerge from the thick forest at Cross Village, a small hamlet and the home of **Legs Inn**.

The inn is the creation of one man, Stanley Smolak, a Polish immigrant who fell in love with this part of Michigan and moved

Petoskey Train Depot, which now houses Little Traverse Historical Museum

here from Chicago in 1921. Smolak quickly made friends with the local Ottawa Indians, who inducted him into their tribe as "Chief White Cloud." Then in 1930, with a Polish past, a love for northern Michigan and his new Indian heritage, Smolak began building the Inn. He combined the driftwood and stones he found along the shoreline to construct an unusual building on a bluff overlooking Lake Michigan. From the outside the architecture of the Legs Inn is bizarre, at best, but the interior is even more fascinating, for Smolak loved to carve the driftwood. He would take a piece, see something in it and then whittle away. The Inn has several rooms, all filled with Smolak's driftwood sculpture.

Naturally the menu reflects Smolak's homeland and includes entrees of pierogi, gotabki, and bigos, a hearty Polish stew. They even serve a beer imported from Poland. The Legs Inn (616-526-

2281) is located in the heart of Cross Village (you'll know it when you see it) and is open May through October from 11 A.M. until midnight, even later on Friday and Saturday, and until 10 P.M. on Sunday. Dinner entrees on the menu range from $9 to $13.

At Cross Village, most traffic turns inland toward US-31, but there is a good reason to split off from the pack and head northeast along Lake Shore Drive. At first the country road gives only views of trees in the Mackinaw State Forest. Eventually, however, it breaks out at the edge of **Bliss Township Park**, situated on Sturgeon Bay, one of the most remote beaches on Lake Michigan. The park itself is little more than four garbage cans and a cement outhouse, but this lonely stretch of beach is one of the few that isn't overrun by hoards of tourists every summer. You can view almost all of Sturgeon Bay from the top of one of the dunes that surround you, and you can scramble down to the shoreline and beachcomb from one end of the bay to the other. Occasionally someone is seen pitching a tent out here, but it's strictly rustic camping.

Otsego County

The Eastern elk, once a common sight to Indians in the Lower Peninsula, disappeared from Michigan around 1877. After several unsuccessful attempts to re-introduce the animal in the early 1900s, seven Rocky Mountain elk were released in Cheboygan County in 1918, and today biologists believe Michigan's herd of 1,100 elk descended from those animals. The herd ranges over 600 square miles in Cheboygan, Montmorency, Otsego, and Presque Isle counties, but its heaviest concentration is in the wilderness areas of the **Pigeon River Country State Forest**.

The 95,000-acre state forest features rustic campgrounds, miles of hiking trails, and fishing opportunities, but come fall most visitors have their hearts set on seeing the elk. As big as the adults are (they range in weight from 700 to 900 pounds), they're tough to spot during the summer, for they break up into small groups or are solitary and lie low in the thick forest. But in September the bulls begin the "bulging season," when they move into open areas and form harems of fifteen to twenty cows by calling out to them with a high pitched whistlelike sound. Elk watchers will see from thirty to a hundred elk gathered in an open field and then witness the most amazing sight—this huge bull making its high-pitched mating call.

To witness one of Michigan's great wildlife scenes, head to the Pigeon River forestry field office, 13 miles east of Vanderbilt, just off of Sturgeon River Road. The office is open from 8 A.M. to 4:30 P.M. Monday through Friday, and workers can provide maps and suggest open areas to view the elk. The rule of thumb is that two weeks on either side of Sept. 20 is the best time to catch the bulging or rutting season. Plan to be at an open area just before dawn or dusk, and sit quietly to await the movement of the herd. One traditional spot to see elk is off of Ossmun Road near its junction with Clark Bridge Road northeast of the forestry office. Here you will find a large open field, a small parking lot off the road, and a few elk viewers waiting patiently during September.

Crawford County

The best-known museum in this county is Hartwick Pines Lumbering Museum, site of one the few virgin stands of white pine that loggers didn't cut at the turn of the century. Within the state park are reproductions of an early logging camp that include the kitchen–mess hall and a workshop. The Interpretive Center recounts the amazing story of Michigan's lumbering era. But after the logging was done much of the state remained as a stump-ridden wasteland. It was the Civilian Conservation Corps (CCC) that replanted the forests, and their story is also told in Crawford County.

The **Civilian Conservation Corps Museum** is located in North Higgins Lake State Park and is dedicated to the program created during President Franklin Roosevelt's administration to help the vast numbers of unemployed men during the Great Depression. It was signed into law as the Emergency Conservation Work Act on March 31, 1933, and by July of that year Michigan had forty-two CCC camps set up that were employing 18,400 men. In all, more than 102,000 Michigan men were enrolled in CCC work projects that involved constructing dams, building hiking trails, stocking lakes, and putting up fire towers. But they are best known for planting trees, and Michigan during the CCC era led the nation in planting 485 million trees.

The museum is composed of several buildings, including an

original cone barn, where workers extracted the seeds from pine cones to later be planted. There is also a replica of a CCC barracks with displays inside that examine the spartan camp life of the men and the duties they performed for $30 a month, of which $22 had to be sent back home to their families. North Higgins Lake State Park (517-821-6125) is reached from US-27 by exiting east on Military Road and from I-75 by heading west at exit 244. There is no admission fee for the CCC museum, but there is a vehicle entry fee for the rest of the park.

Off the Beaten Path in The Heartland

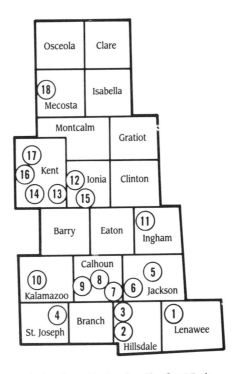

1. Cambridge State Historical Park
2. Allen/Greentop Country Village
3. Litchfield Community Hand Tool Collection
4. Colon/Abbott's Magic Manufacturing Co./Colon Community Museum
5. Jackson/Cascades/Michigan Space Center
6. Mann House in Concord
7. Homer Fire Museum
8. American Museum of Magic in Marshall
9. Binder Park Zoo in Battle Creek
10. Kalamazoo Aviation History Museum
11. Lansing Riverfront Park
12. White's Covered Bridge
13. Fallasburg Covered Bridge
14. Ada Covered Bridge
15. The Roadside Table Historical Site
16. Grand Rapids/Grand Rapids Public Museum/Fish Ladder Sculpture
17. Squires Street Square in Rockford
18. Sawmill Canoe Livery in Big Rapids

The Heartland

By the 1830s, "Michigan Fever" had become an epidemic. Scores of pioneer families from the East Coast floated through the Erie Canal, made their way to Detroit, and then took to the newly completed Detroit–Chicago Road, which cut across the southern half of the Lower Peninsula. They soon discovered the rolling prairies of Michigan, where the soil was very rich and the land very cheap—the federal government was selling it for only $1.25 an acre.

From this onrush of settlers from 1825 to 1855 some of state's largest cities emerged: Kalamazoo, Lansing, Battle Creek, Jackson, and Grand Rapids, all in this central region. But the Heartland of Michigan, the only area without direct links to the Great Lakes, is still an agricultural breadbasket. It is faded red barns and rolling fields of oats, the birthplace of Kelloggs Corn Flakes, and a village antique dealer who scours area farms for the furniture and knickknacks that fill her store.

The vibrant cities, each with a distinct downtown that never sleeps, are popular destinations for travelers who can zip from one to the next on interstate highways, six lanes wide. But the unique nature of this region is found by rambling along its two-lane county roads, which take you past the horse-drawn carriages of Amish country, down main streets of small villages, and along roadside stands loaded with the summer's harvest. In these out-of-the-way places you can sample the fruits of Michigan's Heartland.

Lenawee County

At the northern edge of Lenawee County are the famed Irish Hills, an area of green rolling hills with intermittent lakes and ponds. US-12 cuts through the middle of this popular area and has become an avenue of manufactured tourist attractions: miniature golf courses and go-cart tracks, a dinosaur amusement park, another park called Stagecoach Stop U.S.A., motels, gift shops, and even an international speedway that holds Indy car races. So overwhelming are these modern-day sights that it's easy to pass by one of the most interesting attractions and probably the only one that is free, **Walker Tavern**.

Walker Tavern in Cambridge State Historic Park

Located in Cambridge State Historic Park, the white clapboard tavern overlooks US-12, and rightfully so. The highway was originally an Indian trail and then became a stagecoach route known as the Detroit–Chicago Road. The stagecoach era lasted from 1835 to 1855, and on these rickety wagons, passengers traveled 50 miles a day with the hope of reaching Chicago in five days. The string of frontier taverns along the way were a crucial part of the system. They not only provided overnight accommodations (two or three travelers would share a bed for 25 cents a night) but also meals to the weary passengers who had just spent the day bouncing along the rough dirt road.

By the 1830s Walker Tavern had a reputation as a fine place to dine. Proprietor Sylvester Walker ran not only the inn but a small farm as well, while his wife, Lucy, performed miracles baking in the stone fireplace. A typical supper at Walker Tavern might include stewed chicken, biscuits, corn bread, applesauce cake, and pumpkin pie. The tavern still stands on its original site, and the pub, sitting room, and kitchen have been renovated. Next to the tavern is a reconstructed wheelwright shop, featuring the tools used to build and repair the fragile wooden wheels as well as the covered wagons and carriages of the era. Visitors begin the self-guided walking tour at the Interpretive Center with a film in its theater and an exhibit on the settling of Michigan.

Cambridge State Historical Park (517-467-4414) is on the corner of US-12 and M-50, 25 miles south of Jackson. The tavern complex is open from 10 A.M. to 5 P.M. daily from April 15 through Labor Day and by appointment through October 15.

Hillsdale County

In 1827, a surveying crew for the Detroit–Chicago Road was working in the fertile prairie of the St. Joseph Valley when one member, Captain Moses Allen, fell in love with the area. His homestead led to a small hamlet of homes and shops known as Allen's Prairie, the first white settlement west of Tecumseh. This is the birthplace of Hillsdale County, but today **Allen** is better known as the "Antique Capital of Michigan."

It began as a weekend flea market in the late 1960s that soon drew crowds of antique hunters from several states to the junction of US-12 and M-49. Eventually some of the antique dealers who rented the summer stalls began to set up permanent businesses in Allen. Today this quaint village of fewer than 300 residents supports more than a dozen antique malls, each housing several dealers and other shops along a mile-long stretch of US-12, the town's main street. Some of the shops are located in red brick buildings near the intersection, others in old homes or weathered barns that are packed with furniture and other large antiques.

The largest shop is **Greentop Country Village** (517-869-2100), an antique mall that consists of more than forty dealers displaying their wares in a dozen buildings. The best times to visit Allen are the weekends of Memorial Day, Fourth of July, or Labor Day when the community holds open-air antique festivals and even more dealers converge on the town and set up booths along the streets.

If you are heading south to Allen, swing through the picturesque village of Litchfield 14 miles to the north at the other end of M-49. Near the center of town is the Litchfield Town Hall, and featured in the huge storefront display windows is the **Litchfield Community Hand Tool Collection**. In one window there are seventy-five tools from the turn of the century, in the other another sixty-three, all numbered to correspond to a list taped on the window and in surprisingly good condition. In the three smaller windows on the second floor more tools are hung in display as this town's collection continues to grow and grow. Someday they might have to use all these tools to build a museum for them.

St. Joseph County

Michigan is known for many things, but to the average tourist magicians and magic are not generally one of them. Yet Harry Houdini died in Michigan, and the state has deep roots in the art of illusion and the related conjuring culture. One of the most famous American magicians in the 1920s, Harry Blackstone, toured the country with his act. At one time he passed through the village of Colon and then returned in 1926 and purchased property. Blackstone toured in the winter but spent his summers in Colon creating new illusions and rehearsing his show. One summer Australian magician Percy Abbott came to Colon to visit Blackstone and fell in love with a local girl and the quiet area. Abbott, eager to end his days of traveling, moved to Michigan and formed a partnership with Blackstone to begin a magic manufacturing company.

The partnership went sour after only eight months, but the Australian magician went ahead with his plans and in 1933 set up **Abbott's Magic Manufacturing Company**. Today this sleepy farming village is home for the world's largest magic company, an interesting stop even if you've never done a card trick. The walls inside are plastered with posters and photographs of magicians, for all the famous performers, from Doug Henning to David Copperfield, have done business with this company. There is a display room within the factory, an all-black brick building, with cases and shelves filled with a portion of the 2,000 tricks and gadgets Abbott's Magic builds. And there is always a resident magician on hand to show you how they work.

A year after beginning his company, Abbott also instituted an open house for magicians as a sales incentive, and that quickly evolved into Colon's annual festival, Magical Get-Together. Every August more than a thousand amateur and professional magicians flood the village for a series of shows at the high-school auditorium. Abbott's Magic Manufacturing Company (616-432-3235) is at 124 St. Joseph Street, one block off M-86, and is open from 8 A.M. until 5 P.M. Monday through Friday and until 4:30 P.M. on Saturday.

More magical memorabilia can be viewed at the **Colon Community Museum**, which is housed in an 1893 church at 219 North Blackstone Road. Although many artifacts deal with the town's first pioneer families, one area is devoted to the personal items and photographs of Blackstone and Abbott. The museum (616-432-3672) is open Tuesday, Thursday, and Sunday from 2 to 4:30 P.M. or by appointment. There is no admission.

Jackson County

The Lower Peninsula lacks the waterfalls that grace the countryside in the Upper Peninsula, but in Jackson they have their **Cascades**. Billed as the largest manmade waterfalls in North America, the Cascades were a creation of "Captain" William Sparks, a well-known Jackson industrialist and philanthropist. They date back to the early 1930s, when Captain Sparks was developing a 450-acre park as a gift to the city and wanted it to showcase something different, something no other Michigan city had.

What he developed were the Cascades, a series of eighteen separate waterfalls with water dancing down the side of a hill from one to the next. Six fountains, varying in height and patterns, supply more than 3,000 gallons per minute, while 1,200 colored lights turn this attraction into a nightly event of constantly changing light, color, and music. The total length of the falls is 500 feet, and energetic viewers climb the 129 steps that run along each side of the Cascades, dodging the spray along the way. Others prefer to sit in the amphitheater seats to watch the water and light show that takes place nightly from Memorial Day to Labor Day.

The Cascades (517-788-4320) can be reached from I-94 by taking exit 138 and heading south for 3 miles. Signs point the way to the falls. There is an admission fee.

Michigan Space Center near Jackson

Jackson is home for two U.S. astronauts, Brigadier General James S. McDevitt and Lieutenant Colonel Alfred M. Worden. The two men and all astronauts are honored by the city at the **Michigan Space Center**, located on the Jackson Community College campus. The center is a gold geodesic dome with an 85-foot Mercury Redstone Rocket at its doorstep. More than a dozen other rockets and engines grace the grounds around it, and inside the center visitors can trace the history of space flight from the earliest rockets to a tribute to the *Challenger* disaster. Exhibits include the Apollo 9 Command Module, Mercury and Gemini spaceships, and even the capsule used to carry the first astronauts, chimpanzees.

There is an excellent display on astronaut suits, even the underwear they used and the "bio-harness" they had to wear. Among the hands-on exhibits are a number of helmets visitors can try on, the glove box scientists used to handle lunar specimens, and a scale that will give a person's weight on Mars, Venus, Jupiter, the moon, or for those who care, earth. But perhaps the most intriguing item in the museum is one of the smallest: enclosed in a glass case is a slice from moon rock Number 15555. Around it are photos of astronauts picking it up and maps of its exact location on the moon, but it is the small grayish rock itself, the first piece of the moon most people ever examine, that commands most of the attention.

The Michigan Space Center (517-787-4425) can be reached from I-94 by taking exit 142 (US-127) south 6 miles to the M-50 exit. Turn left on McDevitt, and go 1 mile to the first traffic light; turn left on Hague and follow it 2 miles to Jackson Community College. The center is open from May until September from 10 A.M. to 7 P.M. Monday through Friday, Saturday until 5 P.M., and Sunday from noon to 5 P.M. There is an admission fee, and during the winter the center is closed on Monday.

Ten miles southwest of Jackson is the Victorian town of Concord, the proper setting for the **Mann House**, a Michigan Historical Museum. The three-story house was built in 1883 by Daniel and Ellen Mann, two of the earliest settlers in the area. They raised two daughters, Jessie and Mary Ida, who continued to live in the house and maintained the original furnishings, most dating back to the 1870s. The younger daughter died in 1969 but bequeathed the historic house and all its contents to the people of Michigan through the Michigan Historical Commission.

The house can be toured today, and its eight rooms are a well-preserved trip back to life in the 1880s. The table is set in the dining room; a chess game waits to be played in the parlor; toys, books, and knickknacks fill the children's rooms. As soon as you walk through the wrought-iron gate at the street, you enter an era gone by. The Mann House (517-524-8943) is at 205 Hanover Street in Concord and is open from 10 A.M. to 4:30 P.M. Tuesday through Friday and 1 to 5 P.M. Saturday and Sunday. There is no admission.

Calhoun County

Homer, a small town in the southeast corner of the county, is probably best known for the True Grist Dinner Theater (517-568-4151), which is set in a century-old gristmill on the banks of the Kalamazoo River. After eighty-three years of grinding grain, the mill was restored, right down to the black walnut beams that the U.S. government once attempted to turn into propellers for World War I. Today the huge building is listed on the National Register of Historic Places and provides a unique experience in American dining and professional performances.

Another historic building in Homer, though it's considerably smaller, is a fun place to have breakfast on the Fourth of July: the **Homer Fire Station**. The red brick structure with its arched windows and decorative cornice was built in 1876, five years after Homer was incorporated as a village. It has always been the classic firehall on main street, but in its early days it also served as a jail, town hall, and place for public meetings and local theater performances. It's the oldest building in town, and when Homer decided to replace it they preserved the old firehall by attaching the new fire station to it.

In 1983 it was set up as a museum with donated suits and equipment from former fire fighters. But by far the most impressive item on display had always been there, a horse-pulled steam pumper built in 1887. Homer bought it from Union City in 1904 for $1,200 and placed it in the firehall, where it has been ever since. The best time to see the displays is on the Fourth of July when the town holds its annual Firehall Pancake Breakfast from 7 A.M. until 11 A.M. Almost 500 people enjoy the all-American morning meal in the new fire station with tables set up among the modern equipment. Then they wander into the old hall to see how fires were snuffed out in days past.

The museum does not have regular hours, but those who are passing through may go to the Homer City Offices (517-568-4311) next to the fire station and an employee will open up the museum for you. There is no admission fee.

When Michigan finally became a state in 1837, it was written into the constitution that the capital would be moved from Detroit to a more central location in the Heartland within ten years. Marshall, which was founded in 1830, was so sure it would be chosen that residents donated land along the river for the capitol building, lawyers flocked to the town, and a governor's mansion was built in an area still known as "Capitol Hill." Marshall experienced an economic boom at the possibility of being the political center of the new state. But in 1847, when the state legislature finally was forced to decide the issue, Marshall lost out by a single vote in the Senate to an unprepossessing settlement on the Grand River known as Lansing.

A drive through well-preserved Marshall quickly reveals its rich nineteenth-century heyday; Main Street is lined with storefronts from the 1800s and green historical plaques telling their stories. The houses, especially the renowned Honolulu House, are so intriguing that Marshall's biggest event of the year is its Historical Home Tour in the fall when thousands converge on the city for a walking tour through selected private and public residences. Hidden in all this history and usually left off the travel brochures is Marshall's **American Museum of Magic**.

Located in a restored nineteenth-century storefront with thin Corinthian columns and Victorian-style scalloping, the museum was opened on April Fool's Day (only natural) in 1978 by Bob Lund, a self-professed curator of stage magic history. Three floors contain more than a quarter of a million artifacts and tricks, including 2,700 original posters that decorate the walls, Harry Houdini's submergible escape chamber, and the equipment to perform the saw-the-lady-in-half act. Lund gives a ninety-minute tour of the museum, including trooping to the upper auditorium for some sleight of hand tricks and rabbit pulling from top hats.

The American Museum of Magic (517-781-7674) is open by appointment only, and there is an admission fee.

Battle Creek is best known as the home of Kellogg cereals and as the host of a hot-air balloon festival that draws hundreds of balloonists and thousands of spectators at the Kellogg Regional Airport. But the famous tours through the cereal plants are no longer given, and the balloon festival is not held every year. What you can count on visiting is **Binder Park Zoo**, one of Michigan's most unique displays of fauna and flora.

The zoo is located south of the city in a wooded area along Harper Creek. Instead of a series of cages and animal houses in the middle of a city, Binder Park is a walk through the woods along boardwalks, brick walkways, and wood-chip trails, passing the animal exhibits which have been designed around the existing flora and terrain. There is the Northern Forest Boardwalk where you can view timber wolves, great horned owls and a Sitka deer; a Great Plains area with bison, a prairie dog colony, and snowy owls; hungry trout that you can feed in Harper Creek and a turtle log and viewing area in the pond.

In other areas you will see giant tortoises, zebras, cheetahs, and even a bald eagle, but the most impressive section is Binder's zoo within a zoo. Scheduled to open in 1989 is Miller Children's Zoo, the largest animal contact area in the state. Kids have a chance to feed and touch dozens of animals, including donkeys, rabbits, pygmy goats, draft horses, and pigs. Constructed around these contact stations are intriguing play areas. There's the Pig Pen with models of pigs that children can play on, the Dinosaur Area with a 100-foot-long brontosaurus and fossil-find pit, a giant spider web to climb, and a farm area with a silo slide and cow climber. Circling the entire children's area is the Z.O. & O. Railroad, offering rides on the scaled-down train.

Binder Park Zoo (616-979-1351) is reached from I-94 by taking exit 100 south along Beadle Lake Road and following the signs to the entrance. The zoo is open from mid-April to mid-October from 9 A.M. to 5 P.M. Monday through Friday and until 6 P.M. on Saturday and Sunday. There is an admission fee.

Kalamazoo County

The **Kalamazoo Aviation History Museum** is dedicated to the aircraft of World War II and the role they played in the Allies' success. It's a "living museum," for it not only displays many planes in its hangar on the southeast corner of the city's Municipal Airport, but it restores them to working condition. Visitors are treated to exhibits and historic films in the video room and to a close-up view of a dozen historic planes inside and more planes outside. They can even watch mechanics work on restoring the latest acquisitions.

The musuem has nineteen planes of which fifteen are licensed to fly, and the highpoint of the day is when one is wheeled outside and taken on a short flight around the airport. The times of the flights are posted each day, and people have an opportunity to watch the planes perform and to talk to the pilots afterwards. Planes include a Curtiss P-40 "Flying Tiger" and three Grumman cats—"Wildcat," "Hellcat," and Bearcat"—which led to the museum's nickname, the Air Zoo of Kalamazoo.

The Aviation History Museum (616-382-6555) is at 2101 East Milham Road and is open Monday through Saturday from 10 A.M. to 5 P.M. and Sunday from 1 to 5 P.M. You can drive to the hangar or, if you have your own plane, fly in. There is an admission fee.

Ingham County

One of best urban park developments in Michigan is Lansing's **River Front Park**, or as locals refer to it, RFP. The park is a greenbelt that stretches on both sides of the Grand River from Kalamazoo Avenue just north of I-496 to North Street, 3 miles downstream. A riverwalk, made of long sections of boardwalk near or on the river, runs along the entire east side of the park, with bridges that lead to more walkways and interesting areas on the west side. There are interesting attractions along the park, and you could easily spend an entire day walking from one to the next.

At the south end is the **R. E. Olds Transportation Museum** (517-372-0422), dedicated to the history of transportation in Lansing, where at one time or another fifteen different automobiles were manufactured. Almost twenty cars, from the first Oldsmobile, built in 1897, to an Indy 500 pace car, fill the old City Bus Garage along with old motoring apparel and other memorabilia. The museum is open Tuesday through Friday from 9:30 A.M. until 5 P.M. and Saturday and Sunday from noon to 5 P.M. There is an admission fee.

Right next door is **Impression 5 Museum** (517-485-8116), which is described as an "exploratorium" for children and their parents, stressing hands-on exhibits. The 240 exhibits on several floors range from a music room, filled with unusual instruments to be played, to a touch tunnel where everything is explored using only your tactile sense. Impression 5 is open the same hours as R.E. Olds Museum, and there is an admission fee.

Continuing north along the east side you'll walk under Michigan Avenue and past views of the state capitol, around Sun Bowl Amphitheater and the city's Farmer's Market (open Tuesday, Thursday, and Saturday), and eventually reach **Brenke River Sculpture and Fish Ladder**. The structure is a swirl of steps and stone benches leading down to the fish ladder that curves its way around scenic North Lansing Dam. Come mid-September you can watch salmon and steelhead trout leap from one water ledge of the ladder to the next on their way to spawning grounds.

The park really comes alive during RiverFest, held Labor Day weekend, which includes, among other activities, a lighted boat parade and a fireworks display. But on any clear evening there is a magnificent view of the capitol's lighted dome, shimmering over the Grand River.

Ionia County

When autumn arrives in Michigan and the leaves begin turning shades of red, yellow, and orange, many people instinctively head north to view the fall colors. But the southern portions of the state also enjoy their share of autumn brilliance, and one of the best drives is a 15-mile route that is lined by hardwood forests and rolling farm fields and crosses three covered bridges, including the oldest one in Michigan, **White's Covered Bridge**.

Nestled in a wooded area and spanning the Flat River, White's Covered Bridge was built in 1867 by J.N. Brazee for $1,700 and has faithfully served the public ever since. It is a classic covered bridge with trusses hand hewed and secured with wooden pegs and hand-cut square nails. The bridge is 14 feet wide, 116 feet long, and you can still drive a car across it, though most travelers park on the other side and return on foot for a closer inspection. The bridge is reached by driving to the hamlet of Smyrna in Ionia County (5 miles southwest of Belding) and then heading south on White's Bridge Road.

Continue south on White's Bridge Road for 4 miles, and turn west (left) onto Potters Road for a short distance to Fallasburg Bridge Road, which will lead you over another covered bridge in Fallasburg County Park just inside Kent County. Brazee and his construction company also built the **Fallasburg Covered Bridge**. Its design is similar to White's bridge, and it was built with the same high standards that have allowed both these structures to exist for more than a century. Above both entrances to the Fallasburg Bridge is the stern warning: "$5 Fine For Riding or Driving On This Bridge Faster Than A Walk." The county park is a pleasant stretch of picnic tables and grills on the grassy slopes of the Flat River.

From the park, take Lincoln Lake Avenue south into the town of Lowell and head west on M-21 along the Grand River until you finally cross it into the town of Ada, where signs will point the way to the **Ada Covered Bridge**. The original bridge that crossed the Thornapple River was built in 1867 by Will Holmes but was destroyed by fire in 1980. The residents of Ada immediately opened their hearts (and their wallets), and the bridge was quickly rebuilt and restored. The Ada Bridge is open to pedestrian traffic only.

For those who like obscure historical sites, Ionia County has one of the best in the state. Located on the corner of Morrison Lake Road and Grand River Avenue, south of the town of Saranac, is the place known simply as **The Roadside Table**. It was at this very spot that in 1929 county engineer Allen Williams used a stack of leftover guardrail planks to build a table, the first public picnic table ever placed on a highway right of way. Today, of course, there are roadside tables and rest areas in all fifty states, and the only sights more common on our nation's highways are billboards and McDonald's restaurants. Along the road, the site is marked by only a small white "Historical Site" sign, but a green "State Historic Site" plaque detailing the story has been erected next to the tables. The state still maintains the tables and garbage barrels, even though most of the traffic now flows along I-94 to the south.

Kent County

The favorite son of Grand Rapids is Gerald R. Ford, a local congressman who eventually became the thirty-eighth president of the United States. And although the G.R. Ford Museum, dedicated to his life and his days in office, has only been open since 1981, it is already the city's top attraction. More than a million visitors have passed through the center, which features two floors of exhibits and displays, including a full-scale reproduction of the Oval Office as it appeared in Ford's administration, gifts to the president from other heads of state, and an auditorium that shows the twenty-eight-minute film *Gerald R. Ford—The Presidency Restored.*

But before the Presidential Seal was stamped on this portion of Kent County, Grand Rapids was known as the City of Furniture. In 1853, Grand Rapids was a small frontier town surrounded by forest with a seemingly endless supply of lumber and on the banks of the Grand River, which provided power for the mills. In this setting William "Deacon" Haldane opened a cabinet shop and soon was building not only cupboards but cradles, coffins, and tables and chairs. By the end of the decade there were several shops, and soon "Grand Rapids Made Furniture" became the standard of excellence in household goods.

This history of fine furniture can be traced at the **Grand Rapids Public Museum**, one of the oldest and largest museums in the state. The museum has exhibits of Michigan mammals, archaeology, and Indian artifacts, and one of the most popular sections is the 1890s Gaslight Village. But the heart of the museum is its furniture collection. With more than 1,500 pieces that date from the early 1800s to 1930, it is the largest in the state and one of the top three in the country. A third of the items in the collection were manufactured in Grand Rapids and can be seen in ten "period setting rooms" on the second floor. Even more is displayed at the museum's Voigt House, an 1895 Victorian mansion that still possesses its original furniture.

The Public Museum (616-456-3977) is at 54 Jefferson Avenue Southeast and is open Monday through Saturday from 10 A.M. until 5 P.M. and Sunday from 1 to 5 P.M. There is a small admission fee. Its Voigt House is located nearby at 115 College Avenue Southeast, and tours are given every Wednesday in July and August from 11 A.M. until 3 P.M. and the second Sunday of every month from 1 to 3 P.M. There is also an admission fee for the Voigt House.

When the state began stocking salmon in the Great Lakes in the 1960s, the fish would spawn up the Grand River but had problems getting beyond the Sixth Street Dam in Grand Rapids. The solution was the **Fish Ladder Sculpture**, a unique sculptured viewing area that was designed by local artist Joseph Kinnebrew. Located at 606 Front Street Northwest, just on the north side of I-196, the ladder is a series of seven small ledges on the west bank of the river that allow the salmon to easily leap around the dam. The rest of the sculpture is a platform above the ladder that provides a close view of the large fish as they jump completely out of the water from one ledge to the next.

The first salmon begin arriving in early September, and the run is over in October. Local people say the third week of September is when you'll see the major portion of the spawning run. You won't be the only one there, however, as the river itself will be filled with anglers trying to interest the fish in a lure, a spectacle in itself.

Just 15 miles north of Grand Rapids is the small town of Rockford, which dates back to the 1840s, when a dam and sawmill were built along the banks of the Rogue River. Soon a railroad line passed through Rockford, and the town became a trading center with warehouses, a train depot, mills, and a bean processing plant built along the river. What connected them on land was an unnamed alley that eventually became known as Squires Street. In 1970, the bean plant was renovated into the Old Mill, a cider mill and restaurant. This led to more historical buildings being bought and turned into a strip of specialized shops and stores.

Today **Squires Street Square** is the heart of Rockford, a charming three-block section of more than forty shops and restaurants. You'll find stores in old warehouses, barns, a former shoe factory, a carriage house, even in railroad cars. Rockford Historical Museum occupies the Power House, which sits on the banks of the Rogue River and at one time was a generator plant for a local factory. All the businesses are within walking distance of each other, and most are open Monday through Saturday. Rockford can be reached from US-131 by taking exit 97 and following 10 Mile Road east a short way.

Mecosta County

Big Rapids may be the county seat for Mecosta County, but in recent years the city has also become known as the "Tubing Capital" of Michigan. Owners of **Sawmill Canoe Livery**, which began renting out large truck tubes in 1979, say the portion of the Muskegon River that runs through Big Rapids from their livery to Highbanks Park is the most-tubed waterway in the state, with more than 30,000 people floating down every summer. It's easy to see why on a hot day. Tubing is a lazy and carefree way to beat the heat; you simply place the tube in the water, sit in it, and float. No special skills or paddle strokes are needed.

The run takes about two hours, and tubers often take small coolers (larger ones require their own tube) and plenty of suntan lotion with them. For $3 the livery provides the tube and transportation back from Highbanks Park, and on a hot August day there will be literally hundreds floating along the Muskegon at every bend. Sawmill Canoe Livery (616-796-6408) is at 230 Baldwin Street and rents tubes from May to September.

Off the Beaten Path in the Eastern Upper Peninsula

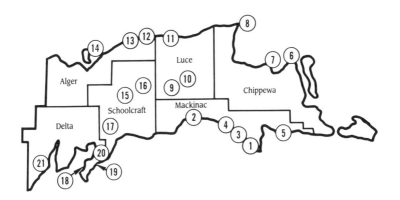

1. Father Marquette National Memorial near St. Ignace
2. Hog Island Point State Forest
3. Lehto's Pasties
4. Cut River Inn
5. Hessel/Les Cheneaux Islands Antique Boat Show
6. Sault Ste. Marie/SS *Valley Camp* Maritime Museum/Locks Park Walkway/Soo Locks Boat Tours/ Antlers
7. Point Iroquois Lightstation
8. Whitefish Point/Great Lakes Shipwreck Museum/Whitefish Point Bird Observatory

9. Helmer House Inn
10. Falls Hotel
11. Muskallonge Lake State Park
12. Lefebvre's Fresh and Smoked Fish Market
13. Grand Sable Banks and Dunes
14. Grand Island Venture
15. Seney National Wildlife Refuge
16. Germfast/Northland Outfitters/ Eagle's Nest Inn
17. Kitch-Iti-Kipi
18. Fayette State Park
19. Portage Bay State Campground
20. Village Artisan's Garden Gallery
21. House of Ludington

Eastern Upper Peninsula

The "Mighty Mac" might sound like a hamburger with the works, but to most Michiganders it's the Mackinac Bridge, the only link between the Lower and Upper peninsulas and the third-longest bridge in the country. Building a bridge was first considered in 1884, but the 5-mile bridge wasn't built until 1957, finally uniting a state that for its first 120 years was divided by a stretch of water known as the Straits of Mackinac.

Most travelers view the Mackinac Bridge as a very scenic drive. A trip across the Mighty Mac is a 360-degree panorama of shorelines, Great Lakes, and islands scattered everywhere, while below the straits bustle with ferries, freighters, and fishing boats. But the bridge is also the link between two worlds. Unlike industrialized southern Michigan, the Upper Peninsula's economy was based on lumbering and mining. After the majestic white pines were cut and the mines closed, this section of Michigan fell upon hard times that continue today. But residents of the north are quick to point out that the first permanent settlement in the state was not Detroit but Sault Ste. Marie, that their endurance proves their long history is not about to end anytime soon. Survival is a way of life in the U.P.

What travelers will quickly discover upon crossing the bridge is a place of remote beauty and unique character, where interstate highways are almost non-existent, motel chains and fast food restaurants few and far between. Almost every road in the U.P. is "off the beaten path," offering natural beauty, family-run inns and cafes, and outdoor opportunities that will satisfy any lover of pristine forests, lakes, and streams.

Mackinac County

The view from Mighty Mac is excellent, but the best view of the bridge itself is from the north shore at **Father Marquette National Memorial**, just outside of St. Ignace. Father Marquette, a newly ordained Jesuit priest from France, paddled his way through the Great Lakes and founded Sault Ste. Marie in 1668, founded St. Ignace three years later, and then joined Louis Jolliet on a 3,000-mile paddle discovering the Mississippi River. He did this—along with converting thousands of Indians to Christianity—in only nine years, dying on the banks of Lake Michigan in 1675.

To celebrate the tricentennial of Marquette's discovery of the Mississippi, a Presidential committee chose St. Ignace as the site of a permanent memorial. Also on the grounds is a museum (open 8 A.M. to 8 P.M. daily June 1 through Labor Day) which includes displays on Marquette and the Indian tribes he encountered, an auditorium with a sixteen-minute film on the life of the priest, and perhaps most intriguing, a replica of the explorer's Mississippi journal in both the original French and English translation. Here you can flip through the pages and read segments of this man's incredible odyssey.

Outside the museum there is an overlook with a public telescope that gives you a sweeping view of the Mackinac Bridge. There are posted exits to the park from both I-75 and US-2.

Scenic shoreline drives abound in Michigan, but it's hard to argue when someone claims the most spectacular of them all is the stretch of US-2 from St. Ignace to the hamlet of Naubinway. The views of Lake Michigan, beaches, dunes, and offshore islands are rarely interrupted in this 42-mile segment. You can drive it in under an hour, or you could spend days stopping at the nine roadside parks, scenic overlooks, and lakeshore campgrounds along the road. One of the campgrounds is **Hog Island Point State Forest**, half hidden between Epoufette Bay and Naubinway and easy to miss if you don't keep an eye out for it. The rustic campground (no electricity or showers) offers sites right on this beautiful shoreline, with sand and surf only a few yards away. The fee is $4 per night.

The north side of the stretch is gradually becoming a row of motels, convenience stores, and cafes—one business little different from the next. But two notable establishments are worth a stop. Some 8 miles west of St. Ignace on US-2 is **Lehto's Pasties**, the first of many pasties shops you are bound to see in the U.P. The Cornish pasty, an Upper Peninsula specialty, looks like a king-size apple turnover crust, but it is filled with meat, potatoes, onion, and a little rutabaga for flavor. They were supper for the miners, who could take the pies down the shafts and at mealtime heat them on their shovels with the candles on their helmets.

Although many believe they originated in the U.P. copper mines in the mid-1800s, they actually date back much earlier to mining days in Cornwall, England.

The lunch counter run by John and Katherine Lehto doesn't look like much, but they have been making pasties since 1947, when John arrived at St. Ignace to take a job on the Straits of Mackinac ferry and his wife opened up the "pasty drive-in." Business was so good that John quit his state job three years later and built the small eatery. Nothing has changed since then—certainly not their pasties, which are hard to beat anywhere in the north. Pasties to go are $2.75 each, and it's an extra dollar if you want to occupy one of the eight seats at the lunch counter. They are open May through November daily from 8:30 A.M. until 6 P.M. or whenever they run out of pasties.

Continue heading west on US-2, and in another 20 miles you'll cross the Cut River Bridge. There are roadside parks on both sides of the structure, because the 641-foot-long bridge is impressive, spanning the gorge of the Cut River, which lies 147 feet below. You can park the car and cross the bridge on foot for a beautiful panorama of Lake Michigan and surrounding shoreline. Or, you can skip the scenery and immediately turn into the **Cut River Inn** on US-2. The inn looks like the typical northwoods bar, with a dozen tables, a stone fireplace in the corner for those chilly winters, and a huge mounted whitetail deer looming over the pool table. But this inn is notable for the way it prepares Great Lake fish. On Friday night the fish fry is perch, but any day of the week you can order whitefish or a U.P. delicacy, menominee, a flaky, white, and almost sweet fillet. The inn also bakes all its own bread and pies and serves a huge hamburger, as any good bar would. The Cut River Inn (906-292-5400) is open year-round Monday through Saturday from 11 A.M. until 10 P.M. and Sunday from noon to 10 P.M. Dinners range in price from $5 to $10.

A much less traveled but equally scenic route is to head east of the Mackinac Bridge on M-134. The road follows the U.P. shoreline along northern Lake Huron, passing intriguing Les Cheneaux Islands and ending at De Tour, the departure point for remote Drummond Island, a haven of fishing resorts. The best stretch is the 24 miles from Cedarville in Mackinac County to De Tour in Chippewa County. This segment is one continuous view of the lake, islands, and long stretches of sand where there are more than a dozen turnoffs and roadside parks, allowing everybody an uncrowded beach for a lazy afternoon in the sun.

The first village M-134 passes through is Hessel, a quaint lakeshore town that comes alive in the first week of August when it is the site of the unusual **Les Cheneaux Islands Antique Boat Show**. The annual festival was started in 1978 because of the large number of wooden hull boats used in the islands, and organizers say it is now the largest gathering of floating antiques in the country. More than 150 vessels, all from the pre-fiberglass era, are displayed in the Hessel marina for close inspection by judges and visitors alike. There is a small admission fee for the one-day event, which includes nautical exhibits, live entertainment, an art festival, and boat excursions around the Les Cheneaux Islands. Call the Les Cheneaux Chamber of Commerce (906-484-3935) in Cedarville for dates and times of the show.

Chippewa County

Sault Sainte Marie is synonymous with the Soo Locks, the world's largest and busiest locking system, the crucial link for freighters passing from Lake Superior to Lake Huron. But the city of 15,000 is Michigan's oldest and has been an important center since the French Canadian voyageurs in the 1700s portaged their long canoes and bales of furs around the St. Mary's Rapids.

Most of this colorful history of shipping can be appreciated by walking along Water Street, beginning at its east end, where the **SS Valley Camp** is docked next to the Chamber of Commerce Information Center. The 550-foot freighter was once owned and used by the Republic Steel Corporation and frequently passed through the locks. Today it has been turned into one of the largest Great Lake marine museums and is listed as a national historic site. From the pilothouse and the 1800-horsepower steam engine to the captain's quarters and the galley, visitors are free to roam the ship for a close-up look at life aboard an ore carrier, where a crew of almost thirty worked, slept, and ate. Down below, in its massive cargo holds, are models and displays of Great Lake vessels, aquariums of the freshwater fish that abound nearby, and a room devoted to wreckage of the *Edmund Fitzgerald*, the ore carrier that sank in the raging Lake Superior in 1975, taking its captain and crew of twenty-eight with it.

The SS *Valley Camp* (906-632-3658) is open daily from 10 A.M. to 5 P.M. May 15 to June 30; 9 A.M. to 8 P.M. July 1 to Aug. 31; and 10 A.M. to 5 P.M. Sept. 1 Oct. 16. There is an admission fee.

109

To reach the locks to the north, follow Water Street, which in 1982 was renovated into the **Locks Park Walkway**, providing an excellent overview of the city's 350-year past. The walkway is marked by blue symbols of freighters, and interpretative plaques explain the history of various areas and renovated buildings. Along the way you'll pass the Baraga House, the 1864 home of missionary and historian Bishop Frederic Baraga, the "Snowshoe Saint" and first bishop of the U.P. Nearby is the Johnston House, which was constructed in 1794 for an Irish fur trader, making it the oldest surviving home in Michigan. The walkway also passes the site of Fort Brady, built by the Americans in 1823, and the spot where in 1820 General Lewis Cass lowered and removed the last British flag to fly over U.S. soil.

Water Street ends at Soo Lock Park in the heart of downtown Sault Sainte Marie. The U.S. Army Corps of Engineers maintains the park and visitor center, and next to the locks they built a raised viewing platform that provides an excellent view of ships being raised and lowered to the different lake levels. You can experience the locks directly through **Soo Locks Boat Tours**. For an admission fee, people take a two-hour cruise up and down the St. Mary's River, first passing through an American Lock and then returning through the Canadian one. Boats depart daily from May 15 through Oct. 15, beginning at 9 A.M. and ending with the last cruise at 5:30 P.M. Soo Locks Boat Tours (906-632-2512) maintains two docks, both on Portage Avenue south of the SS *Valley Camp*.

As well known to locals as the locks is **The Antlers**, an Irish bar and restaurant on Portage Avenue. The exterior of the simple stone building that houses the seventy-year-old eatery is misleading. Inside, the decor is a museum of collectibles (or some say junk), including hundreds of mounted animals on the walls, a birch bark canoe hanging from the ceiling, and a 15-foot boa constrictor overlooking the bar. No wall is left bare. Hockey great Gordie Howe (whose picture also adorns the walls) was a frequent patron of the restaurant, which is known for its steaks and "Paul Bunyan" hamburgers. The Antlers (906-632-3571) is open daily from 11 A.M. to 10 P.M., and dinner prices range from $6 to $15.

One of the more interesting drives in the U.P. follows Whitefish Bay, beginning at Brimley (reached from M-28) and ending at desolate Whitefish Point. At Brimley follow Lake Shore Drive to the west as it hugs the shoreline, with frequent views of beaches

**Point Iroquois Lightstation Museum on Lake
Superior**

and Lake Superior. In 7.5 miles, you'll come to **Point Iroquois
Lightstation**. The classic lighthouse was built in 1870 and operated until 1963 when sophisticated radar made it obsolete. The
Coast Guard turned it over to the U.S. Forestry Service, which
worked with local historical societies to open it up to the public
in 1984. It has since been added to the National Register of Historic Places and features a few displays and artifacts in three
rooms of the lightkeeper's house. But this lighthouse is mostly
popular for its climbing curved stairwell of 70 steps that leads to
the top of the tower and a view of the surrounding area. The
panorama, needless to say, is impressive, as you can see almost
the entire coastline of Whitefish Bay and miles out into Lake
Superior, including any freighter that happens to be passing by.
The lightstation is open year-round from 10 A.M. until 5 P.M. and
from 7 to 9 P.M. daily.

Lake Shore Drive, with its numerous pulloffs and scenic
beaches, ends when it merges into M-123. The state road is well
traveled, as it first heads north along the shoreline of Whitefish

Bay and then at Paradise swings west to head inland to Tah-quamenon Falls. The popular falls, the second largest east of the Mississippi River (Niagara Falls is the largest), is the destination for most travelers. But there is a good reason to continue heading north on Whitefish Point Road. At the very end of the road, at the very tip of the remote peninsula that juts out into Lake Superior, is the **Great Lakes Shipwreck Museum**. Whitefish Point is a combination of sandy beach, small dunes, and thunderous Lake Superior waves crashing along the shoreline. It also marks the east end of an 80-mile stretch that sailors knew as the "Grave-yard of the Great Lakes." Raging northwest storms, built up over 200 miles of open water, have caused 300 recorded shipwrecks along this section of shoreline, in which 320 seamen have died.

The Great Lakes Shipwreck Historical Society, a group of divers researching the wrecks, opened the museum in 1986 in aban-doned buildings of the Coast Guard Station whose light, beaming since 1849, is the oldest active one on Lake Superior. In the main museum, each display is devoted to a different shipwreck. See a drawing or photograph of the vessel and artifacts that divers have collected, and read the story of its fatal voyage. The ships range from sailing schooners of the early 1800s to the *Edmund Fitzgerald*, the latest and largest shipwreck, which continues to fascinate residents of the U.P. A darkened interior with theatrical lights, soft music, and special sound effects of sea gulls and fog horns sends tingles down the spines of most visitors.

Another building has been turned into a theater where under-water films of the wrecks are shown, and eventually the light-keeper's house will be open to visitors. The museum is open from Memorial Day until mid-October daily from 10 A.M. to 6 P.M. There is an admission fee. Most of the point is a state wildlife sanctuary, renowned for the variety of birds that pass through. The Michigan Audubon Society has established the **Whitefish Point Bird Ob-servatory**, across from the lightstation, where a small informa-tion room tells birders the species to be watching for as they hike along the network of trails along the point.

Luce County

The county that lies between Chippewa and Alger is probably best known for the Two Hearted River, fished by Ernest Hemingway and later the setting for one of his stories. Today it remains a favorite for anglers and canoers who enjoy the solitude of this remote wilderness river that empties into Lake Superior.

For travelers in Luce County who want to spend their nights in comfort at an inn or hotel, there are two interesting places, well worth the out-of-the-way drive to reach them. One is the **Helmer House Inn**, located on the northeast corner of Manistique Lake near the Luce-Mackinac county line. To reach it, you head north from US-2 on County Road H-33 and then swing onto County Road 417. The inn was built in 1881 by a minister as a mission for early settlers; Gale Helmer turned it into a general store and resort six years later. The area thrived as a summer getaway, so the federal government set up a post office in the inn, appointed Helmer postmaster, and named the spot, for a lack of a better name, Helmer.

The post office lasted only nineteen years and eventually the building was abandoned. Rob Goldthorpe and his wife renovated the lodge and reopened it in 1982. Today the inn is a state historic site, and offers five guest rooms, all furnished with antiques. The lodge is probably better known, however, for its wraparound porch that was glassed in and turned into a delightful little restaurant. Every table has a view of the rural setting outside, and the menu includes steaks, fish, and occasionally stuffed trout. The small salad bar is excellent.

Overnight guests are treated to a full breakfast in the morning as well as a soft bed at night. Rooms, which have shared bathrooms, range from $14 to $32 for singles or doubles. The restaurant is open from noon to 9 P.M. daily except Tuesday, with dinner prices from $5 to $11. For room reservations write to the Helmer House Inn (906-586-3204) at McMillan, MI 49853.

Also known more for its meals than its rooms is the **Falls Hotel** in Newberry on M-123. The hotel was built on the edge of Newberry in 1915 after the only inn in town burned down. Although it was on the outskirts of town, the hotel was the social center of the community, and eventually Newberry's entire business district relocated around it from nearby Helen Street. The Falls Hotel (906-293-5111) is a state historic site known by travelers for its restaurant—especially the smorgasbord, which includes freshly caught whitefish, menominee, or other delicacies from Lake Superior. The smorgasbord is served daily from mid-June until Labor day, and the restaurant is open from 11 A.M. until 9 P.M. Dinner prices range from $6 to $13.

The other pleasant spot in Luce County to spend a night is **Muskallonge Lake State Park** at the north end of County Road H-37 in the northwest corner of the county. The park is actually a strip of land lying between Muskallonge Lake, known for its pike, perch, and small mouth bass fishing, and Lake Superior. You can camp on a site overlooking the small lake and then wander over to Lake Superior to enjoy its seemingly endless sandy shoreline. There is a vehicle fee to enter Muskallonge Lake State Park (906-658-3338) and an overnight fee of $8 for one of its 179 campsites.

Alger County

Pasties are the best-known dish U.P. cooks serve, but another delicacy of the north is smoked fish. Driving the shoreline roads along Lake Superior you'll see a number of smokehouses offering whitefish, lake trout, herring, and menominee, but no one does it better than Vern Kirkens of Grand Marais. Kirkens has been smoking fish since the early 1960s and today runs **Lefebvre's Fresh & Smoked Fish Market** located in town off H-58. Kirkens says the best fish is smoked with hardwood (he uses sugar maple), but that some houses try to cut costs by using mostly propane. If you have never eaten smoked fish, first try lake trout, which has a much more delicate flavor than whitefish or herring. Break off large chunks and enjoy them with a bit of sharp cheddar cheese on a slice of dark bread while sipping an ice-cold beer on the sandy shoreline of Grand Marais. Many think it's the Upper Peninsula at its finest.

The Lefebvre Fresh & Smoked Fish Market (906-494-2563) is open from 9 A.M. until 9 P.M. daily from mid-May until early December. The shop also sells smoked turkey, homemade beef jerky, and pies, turnovers, and sticky cinnamon buns that Kirkens's wife bakes daily.

Grand Marais, a booming lumbertown of 2,500 at the turn of the century, is a sleepy hamlet of 400 today and the gateway for the eastern half of Picture Rocks National Seashore. The National Park Service maintains the Grand Marais Ranger Station and Maritime Museum (906-494-2669) near the harbor. It provides maps and information on the park along with a sailor's history of the area. One spot they will undoubtedly urge you to see within the park is the **Grand Sable Banks and Dunes**.

To reach the sandy hills, follow County Road H-58 west of town, first passing the parking lot and short side trail to Sable Falls and then the Grand Sable Visitor Center. From both places there are half-mile trails that lead to the Grand Sable Dunes. Or you can continue following the county road a mile past the visitor's center until the pavement ends. On one side of the road is the picnic area and beach of Grand Sable Lake, and on the other side is a huge dune. There are no more than 50 yards between the lake and this mountain of sand. Visitors first tackle the heart-pounding scramble up the dune, where at the top there's a magnificent view of the wind-swept sand, Grand Sable Lake, and Lake Superior off in the distance. Then it's a mad dash down the steep bank of sand and usually right into the lake to cool off.

The dunes are a 4-square-mile area of sandy hills about half as high as Sleeping Bear Dunes in the Lower Peninsula, but no less impressive. They end with the Grand Sable Banks, steep sandy bluffs that tower right above the Lake Superior shoreline, some 300 feet tall. The best view is obtained by turning off H-58 onto a marked side road for the log slide located 8 miles west of Grand Marais. A short boardwalk leads to a breathtaking overlook 300 feet above Lake Superior where to the west Au Sable Point Lighthouse is silhouetted against the water while to the east the banks curve 5 miles back toward Grand Marais. Down below is the 500-foot wooden slide that loggers used in the 1800s to send trees into Lake Superior on their way to town. The lighthouse, which was built in 1874, has been renovated by the National Park Service and is an easy 1.5-mile hike from Hurricane River Campground located farther west on H-58.

You could continue along H-58, although only about half of it is paved, and end up in Munising. The scenic town is the gateway to the Picture Rocks, sandstone cliffs that rise 50 to 200 feet above Lake Superior and stretch for 15 miles to the west. They are one of the top attractions in the U.P., and during the summer visitors take a Picture Rock cruise or drive to its most famous formation, Miner's Castle. But Munising is also on the edge of another park, the Alger Underwater Preserve, a graveyard of shipwrecks that date back to the 1800s and early 1900s.

The preserve and especially the waters around Grand Island are a haven for scuba divers who view the wrecks that lie 10 to 100 feet below the surface. But non-divers can also enjoy the treasures of Lake Superior with **Grand Island Venture**, a charter service out of Munising. Captain Peter Lindquist takes snorkelers into the preserve, where they can view a number of wrecks, including the *Dreadnaught*, a three-mast schooner that lies off Grand Island only 10 feet below the surface. The ship, which dates back to the 1880s, is still intact with a complete hull. Other wrecks lie 20 to 30 feet below the surface, but in Lake Superior's crystal clear water, even snorkelers can get a good view of them.

The cost is $15 per person for each wreck; a two-wreck trip lasts two and a half hours. Often wet suits are not necessary for the swims, but if additional warmth is needed, the suits can be rented next door at Sea & Ski Scuba (906-387-2927). You can write to Grand Island Venture (906-387-4477) at Mill Street, Route 1, P.O. Box 436, Munising, MI 49862.

Schoolcraft County

The heart of Schoolcraft County, some 96,000 acres, has been preserved as the largest wildlife refuge east of the Mississippi River. The **Seney National Wildlife Refuge** was established in 1935 by the U.S. Fish and Wildlife Service to provide a habitat for wildlife, primarily waterfowl migrating to nesting grounds in Canada. The refuge surrounds the Great Manistique Swamp, which endured rough treatment beginning in the 1870s when loggers were intent on stripping every tree from the area. Fires were then deliberately set to clear away the debris of the lumbering operation, preventing new forests from taking root. Finally a land development company came through, drained acre after acre of the swamp, and sold the land to farmers for agriculture in 1911. The farmers lasted about a year, discovering they had been swindled—the soil would grow little.

Seney was now a wasteland that nobody wanted. The state ended up with it, and during the Great Depression deeded it to the federal government with the recommendation that it be turned into a refuge. Civilian Conservation Corps workers came in and built dikes, dug ditches, and used other water control devices to impound 7,000 acres of water in twenty-one major ponds, almost miraculously restoring the marsh. Seney again became a habitat for waterfowl when 332 Canada geese were released in 1936 and established its present nesting flocks. Still more geese and other species of birds depend on the area as an important rest stop on their long migration to nesting sites in Canada.

Other wildlife—timber wolves, deer, black bears, moose, and coyotes—live in the refuge, but the Canada goose has clearly become the symbol of Seney's return to wilderness. You will see the "honkers" the minute you drive into the parking lot of the Visitor's Center, as a few tame ones are always around looking for a handout from soft-hearted tourists. The center overlooks one of the many ponds in the refuge, and a telescope at its large viewing window lets you search the marsh area for some of the more than 200 species of birds that can be found in the area. The center has displays, a children's touch table, and an auditorium that hosts nature movies and slide programs each hour. It is open from May 15 through Sept. 30 from 9 A.M. until 5 P.M. daily.

But the best way to view the wildlife is to follow the 7-mile Marshland Wildlife Drive in your car as it winds its way among the ponds, starting near the center and ending at M-77 just south of the refuge entrance. Pick up a free guide that points out items of interest at a number of marked stops, including an active bald eagle nest that can be seen clearly from the drive. Timing is important for spotting wildlife, and it is best to follow the drive either in early morning or at dusk when the animals are most active. Often during the peak of the tourist season the refuge will stage guided evening tours that depart around 6 P.M. and last for almost two hours. Call the visitor's center (906-586-9851) for information regarding the auto tours.

Another unique way to view more remote areas of the refuge is to paddle the handful of rivers that flow through it. **Northland Outfitters** (906-586-9801) is located in nearby Germfask and offers canoe rentals for the area. The outfitters will supply canoes, paddles, life jackets, and transportation to the Manistique River, which runs through the southeast corner of Seney. The trips are self-guided, last either two or four hours, and offer the possibilities of spotting beaver, deer, otters, or a variety of birds or of fishing for walleye or pike in the river. Next to the outfitters is **Eagle's Nest Inn**, a restaurant housed in one of the original refuge buildings constructed in the late 1930s. The inn now looks like a Cape Cod–style eatery and specializes in whitefish, perch, and lake trout from the Great Lakes. Hours are 11:30 A.M. until 8 P.M. daily except Monday from mid-April through November. Dinners range from $10 to $16.

On the opposite scale of parks is Palms Brook, a state park of only 388 acres located 12 miles northwest of Manistique on M-149. the park may be small but it's equally intriguing due to **Kitch-Iti-Kipi**, Michigan's largest spring. The natural spring pours out more than 10,000 gallons of water per minute from fissures in the underlying limestone and has created a crystal clear pool 200 feet wide and 40 feet deep. Visitors board a wooden raft with observation holes in the middle and pull themselves across the spring to get a good view of the fantasy world below. Between the swirls of sand and ghostly bubbles rising up, you can view ancient trees with branches encrusted in limestone, huge brown trout slipping silently by, and colors and shapes that challenge the imagination. The spring is especially enchanting in the early morning, when a mist lies over the water and the trout rise to the surface. Palms Brook has a picnic area but no campsites, and there is a vehicle fee to enter. The raft is free.

Delta County

In the mid-1800s, iron ore was shipped from the Upper Peninsula mines to the foundries in the lower Great Lakes at a tremendous cost to companies. The high price of shipping was due to the inefficient method of transportation coupled with the nearly 40 percent waste the ore contained. Fayette Brown, general manager of the Jackson Iron Company, studied the problem and decided the solution was to build a company-owned furnace not far from the mine where the ore could be smelted into pig iron before it was shipped to the steel-making centers. The town he planned to build had to be a reasonable distance from the Escanaba ore docks, possess a natural harbor, and be near large amounts of limestone and hardwood forests that were needed to smelt the iron ore. In 1866, Brown chose a spot on the Garden Peninsula overlooking Big Bay De Noc, and the town of Fayette was born.

A year later the work began on the furnace and charcoal kiln, and by Christmas the first iron from Fayette was cast. Quickly a town emerged. There was the superintendent's house on a bluff overlooking the harbor, a company office, nine frame dwellings for the engineers and skilled workers, forty log cabins for the unskilled laborers. Eventually Fayette featured a machine shop, small railroad, barns, blacksmith shop, hotel, and even an opera

Charcoal Kiln in Fayette Historical State Park

house. It was a total community that in 1884 had a population of almost 1,000 and turned out 16,875 tons of iron. But toward the end of that decade, Fayette's fate was sealed. The price of pig iron fell, and newly developed coke blast furnaces produced a higher quality iron at a much cheaper rate. In 1891, the company closed down the furnaces and within a few years Fayette became a ghost town.

Fayette changed hands several times; at last the state of Michigan obtained the area in 1959 and turned it into **Fayette State Park**. The town booms again as a scenic ghost town overlooking Snail Shell Harbor, with its towering white cliffs. The 365-acre park is reached from US-2 on County Road 483 and contains an interpretative museum with information, guide maps, and a scale model of Fayette during its heyday. From there you leisurely wander through twenty-two existing buildings, of which nine are open. The renovated structures, which are furnished, include the company office, the hotel, the opera house, and a home of one of the skilled employees. More will be opened up in the future.

Fayette State Park (906-644-2603) also has eighty campsites, a beach and picnic area, and boat-launching facilities. The museum is open daily from April through October from 9 A.M. until 6 P.M. There is a vehicle fee to enter the park and an $8-per-night fee to camp.

Two other spots are worth searching out on Garden Peninsula. One is **Portage Bay State Campground**, which is reached from County Road 483 (before the state park) by turning off on County Road 08 and carefully following the signs. The rustic campground (no electricity, pit toilets) is a bumpy 5-mile ride along dirt roads, but the camping area is worth it: You pitch your tent or park your trailer among the pine trees that border the sandy beach of the bay. You can stroll along the beach, follow the hiking trails in the area, or take a dip in the clear water of Lake Michigan.

The last town you pass through before reaching the state park is Garden, and right in the middle of the village on County Road 483 is **Village Artisan's Garden Gallery** (906-644-2205). The gallery features two rooms of pottery, hand-knit sweaters, dolls, jewelry, and other work from more than fifty area artists. The quaint little shop is open during the summer on Friday from 1 to 5 P.M., Saturday from 10 A.M. to 5 P.M., Sunday from 1 to 5 P.M., or whenever Ginny Smith is in.

Escanaba, the third-largest city in the U.P. with a population of more than 14,000, is situated on the shores of scenic Little Bay De Noc. The bay can best be enjoyed from the city's Ludington Park, which stretches almost 1.5 miles along it. The park contains a picnic area, bike trails, Delta County Historical Museum (open 1 to 9 P.M. daily during the summer), a yacht club, a band shell with regularly scheduled events, and Aronson Island. The island, connected to the main park by a bridge, is a pleasant spot with sandy beaches, nice views of the inner harbor, and plenty of spots for a shore fisherman to wet a line.

The park ends to the north at the city's Visitor's Bureau, and across the street is the **House of Ludington**, a magnificent white hotel with green awnings and medieval-looking cupolas. The building was constructed in 1883, and its rooms have been booked by such guests as John Philip Sousa, Henry Ford, Guy Lombardo, and even such contemporary celebrities as NFL quarterback Lynn Dickey and singer Johnny Cash. Its restaurant is renowned in the city, and there isn't a better way to view Ludington Park than to book a ride on the classic horse and carriage that is parked at the front doors from 6 to 11 P.M. daily in the summer. Rooms at the House of Ludington (906-786-4000) range from $40 to $68 per night.

Off the Beaten Path in the Western Upper Peninsula

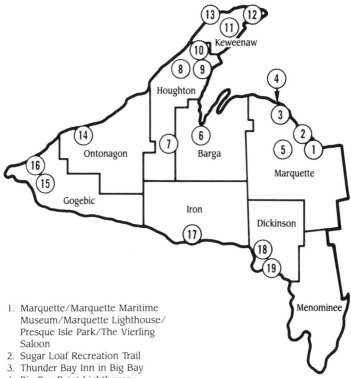

1. Marquette/Marquette Maritime Museum/Marquette Lighthouse/Presque Isle Park/The Vierling Saloon
2. Sugar Loaf Recreation Trail
3. Thunder Bay Inn in Big Bay
4. Big Bay Point Lighthouse
5. Michigan Iron Industry Museum near Negaunee
6. Hilltop Restaurant south of L'Anse
7. Sturgeon River Gorge Area
8. Library Bar and Restaurant
9. Lindell's Chocolate Shop
10. Calumet/Calumet Opera House/ Shulte's Bar
11. Delaware Mine
12. Brockway Sauna in Copper Harbor
13. Sand Dune Drive
14. Porcupine Mountains Wilderness State Park
15. Black River Harbor Drive
16. Bear Track Inn
17. Iron Country Museum
18. The Stables
19. Pier Gorge and the Roaring Rapids Raft Co.

Western Upper Peninsula

Michigan's most remote and rustic region is the rugged western Upper Peninsula. Two small ranges located here constitute the only true mountains in any of the Great Lakes states; between Baraga and Marquette lie the Huron Mountains, and along the Lake Superior shoreline, from west of Ontonagon to Copper Harbor, is the Copper Range. Within these rugged hills is Mount Curwood, the highest point in Michigan at 1,998 feet above sea level, and the Porcupine Mountains, between whose ridges and peaks lies the stunning Lake of the Clouds.

It was in these hills of the western U.P. that the great iron and copper mines flourished from the 1800s to the 1940s, bringing boatloads of immigrants from Norway, Finland, and Italy to work in the shafts. Today the remnants of the mining era are ghost towns, abandoned mines, and communities with strong ethnic heritage and pride.

For most Michigan residents, this region of the state is a remote, distant place; driving to Copper Harbor from Detroit is the same distance as traveling to Washington, D.C. But once it is "discovered," travelers marvel at the western U.P.'s natural wonders. More than for its mines, pasty shops, and historical museums, you come to this region of Michigan for the beauty of nature's handiwork: cascading waterfalls, panoramas of forested wilderness, a lake set in a sea of reds, yellows, and oranges painted by autumn leaves.

Marquette County

The largest county in Michigan includes 1,873 square miles, 1,800 lakes, 73 miles of Lake Superior shoreline, and Marquette, the largest (and some say, only) city in the Upper Peninsula. The city of 23,000 became a spot on the map with a post office in 1849, and it bloomed the following decade as the port and shipping center for the nearby iron mines and logging camps. The lumber and mining barons graced the streets of Marquette with mansions, many still standing today. From Front Street turn east onto Ridge Street and you'll head toward Lake Superior, passing one late Victorian home after another until you end up in the parking lot of the **Marquette Maritime Museum** on the waterfront.

The museum is housed in the red sandstone Old Water Works Building and features displays on shipwrecks, antique outboard motors and boats, commercial fishermen who worked the area, and other facets of the city's maritime days, which fed many and made some (from the looks of their homes) incredibly wealthy. Open from Memorial Day until Sept. 30, the museum can be viewed from 11 A.M. until 5 P.M. Tuesday through Sunday. A small admission fee is charged. More maritime history can be seen next door at the **Marquette Lighthouse**, built in 1866 and still in operation today under the careful eye of the U.S. Coast Guard. The picturesque lighthouse, a bright red structure, sits on a high bluff called Lighthouse Point, which offers a sweeping view of the city's waterfront. The lighthouse (906-226-3312) is open to the public, but visitors are asked to first register at the Coast Guard office.

The largest and most interesting structures on Marquette's waterfront are the iron ore docks that load the Great Lakes freighters with the rock for a journey south. There are two interesting places in town to view them. The Lake Superior and Ishpeming Railroad docks are still operating today, and the best vantage point is **Presque Isle Park**. The 328-acre city park is not an isle but a peninsula that juts out into Lake Superior on the north side of Marquette. A road circles the park shoreline, beginning on the south side, where you can see the ore docks and, if your timing is right, watch a freighter receive its load (one to three times a week).

The drive continues and passes the steep red cliffs of Lookout Point and then the view at Sunset Point where residents gather to watch the end of another day. The park also has an outdoor band shell with weekly events, a small zoo, a beach and bathhouse, picnic areas, and bicycle paths. Hiking trails crisscross the forested interior of Presque Isle and become a favorite spot for nordic skiers during the winter. The park is open daily from 7 A.M. until 11 P.M., and perhaps the best time of year to visit it is the last weekend in July during its Art-on-the-Rocks Festival when local artists gather to display and sell their work in this picturesque setting.

In Marquette's Lower Harbor is the Old Ore Docks, no longer operating, which has been designated a state historic site. An excellent place to view the docks is from a table in **The Vierling Saloon** on the corner of Front and Main Streets. The saloon was opened in 1883 by Martin Vierling, an art lover and saloon keeper who headed north with his paintings after running an establishment in Detroit. Later the art lover's bar became just another cafe during prohibition, but the present proprietors, Terry and Christi Doyle, have turned back the clock by renovating the interior and returning the building to its original function as a saloon and fine restaurant. The brick walls inside once again feature paintings and prints, as the owners exhibit an artist every month. There are also old photographs and artifacts of early Marquette, and the large windows in the rear of the restaurant overlook the iron ore docks. A pair of binoculars hangs on the back wall for anyone wanting a closer look at the massive structure.

The menu is "geared to healthy food," and the dinner menu features several shrimp and chicken entrees and Rogan Josh, an Indian spiced red stew served with yellow rice and chutney. The Vierling Saloon is open daily except Sunday from 7 A.M. until 9:30 P.M. Dinner is served after 4 P.M., and prices range from $7 to $10.

For an excellent view of all of Marquette head north of town on County Road 550 for a few miles and turn into the dirt parking lot marked by the large Sugar Loaf sign. This is the start of the **Sugar Loaf Recreational Trail**, a wide and easy path that winds 0.6 mile up the peak of the same name. You actually climb 315 feet through forest and over granite ridges by a series of steps until you reach the rocky knob marked by a stone monument. The view is spectacular on a clear day, a 360-degree panorama that includes the city, Lake Superior, the rough coastline, and the many islands that lie offshore.

By continuing north on County Road 550 for another 26 miles, you reach its end in the small village of Big Bay on the shores of Lake Independence. Big Bay is best known as a place where scenes for the film *Anatomy of a Murder*, starring Jimmy Stewart and Lee Remick, were filmed. The story is true, though the murder really took place at Lumberjack Tavern, a classic northwoods bar that was later used for one scene in the movie. Other footage was taken in the Big Bay Hotel, which is now the **Thunder Bay Inn**.

The large inn was built in 1911 as a company store and warehouse and then turned into a hotel. In 1943, Henry Ford purchased it along with the mill at the north end of the lake to produce the wooden parts for his cars. The industrialist exten-sively remodeled the hotel and literally reshaped the landscape in front of it. So obsessed was Ford with being able to see his fac-tory from his hotel that he had the town's railroad depot moved and County Road 550 re-routed. It was in 1958, under different owners, that several short scenes of the famous murder mystery were filmed in the hotel's lobby, dining room, and bedrooms up-stairs. Eventually the facility was abandoned and sat empty for ten years.

In 1985, Darryl Small bought the hotel and opened the first of twelve rooms two years later. Today the large inn is an interesting place to stay or have dinner. All the rooms have been renovated (you can even stay in Ford's Room), and guests begin their day with coffee and rolls served on the second floor balcony that is furnished with wicker and overlooks the lake and, yes, Ford's old factory. Room rates for double occupancy range from $45 to $55 and include tours of Lake Superior in the hotel's vessel *Bonnie Lass*. For reservations call (906-345-9977) or write Thunder Bay Inn, P.O. Box 286, Big Bay, MI 49808.

Another equally interesting place to stay in the area is the **Big Bay Point Lighthouse**, the secluded retreat located 3.5 miles north of town on Lighthouse Road. The light at Big Bay was built and put into service in 1896 and included a two-story, red brick dwelling with eighteen rooms. The house was divided in half, with the lightkeeper residing in one half and his assistant in the other. The U.S. Coast Guard automated the light in 1941 and then sold it in 1961 after building a new steel tower nearby.

Buck Gotschall became the second private owner of the light-house and in 1986 opened it as a unique bed and breakfast offer-ing guests the rare opportunity to stay overnight at a lighthouse in one of its six bedrooms. The light stands high above Lake Superior on a rocky point in the middle of forty wooded acres that include 2 miles of trails. You can climb the narrow staircase to the top of the tower for a splendid view of the area, catching a sunrise over Lake Superior at daybreak, a sunset over the Huron Mountains at dusk, or possibly the Northern Lights at night. The interior has been completely renovated and refinished, showing its natural wood and brick, and the various rooms include, among others, a delightful sauna.

The lighthouse (906-345-9957) is open year-round with special rates for the off season, weekdays, and package stays. The basic rate for the summer ranges from $59 to $89 for rooms that sleep from two to four persons. For reservations write Lighthouse, #3 Lighthouse Road, Big Bay, MI 49808.

The newest Michigan Historical Museum is tucked away in the woods near Negaunee and is probably passed up by many visitors. That's a shame, for the **Michigan Iron Industry Museum** is an interesting stop that allows you to leisurely explore the history of the Upper Peninsula's iron industry. The museum lies in the forested ravines of the Marquette Iron Range and overlooks Carp River, where the first iron forge in the Lake Superior region was built in 1848. The U.P.'s iron deposits had been discovered four years earlier when William Burt, leading a U.S. Survey party near the area, noticed the magnetic needle of his compass jumping wildly about. He instructed his men to search the ground, and immediately they turned up outcrops of almost pure iron among the roots of pine trees. The iron era of the U.P. had begun, and in 1846 Jackson Mine, the first operation in the U.P., was opened near Negaunee.

The museum, dedicated in May of 1987, does an excellent job of leading you through the history of iron, from its beginnings to its most robust era to the decline of the industry in the 1960s. Inside there are several levels of displays, a reconstructed mine shaft to walk through, and an auditorium that presents a short introductory program. Outside are more artifacts, including a mine locomotive, and trails lead to the old forge site on Carp River. The museum is reached from US-41 by turning onto County Road 492 3 miles east of Negaunee and is open daily from 9:30 A.M. until 4:30 P.M. from mid-May until mid-October. Admission is free.

Baraga County

Although serious research has never been done, many say the largest and best sweet rolls in the state are found at the **Hilltop Restaurant**, on US-41 just south of L'Anse. One roll is an ample breakfast for most people since it measures more than 5 inches across and 3 inches thick and arrives filled with cinnamon and dripping in glaze. The restaurant is operated by Judy Jaeger and Vivian Delene, but its sweet roll fame was already established when they purchased the business in 1975. On a good weekend they will serve more than a thousand. The eatery also has other items on its menu (including good pasties), but who has room for anything else after devouring its sticky specialty with a cup of fresh-brewed coffee. The Hilltop is open from 6 A.M. to 8 P.M. daily.

Houghton County

One of the most spectacular areas of the U.P.'s interior is relatively unknown to travelers who are hesitant to leave paved roads. The **Sturgeon River Gorge Area** is located just inside Houghton County along its border with Baraga County south of M-38. The wilderness area includes the gorge cut by the Sturgeon River, which in some places is more than 400 feet deep, making it the largest and deepest in the Great Lakes states. For the best view of it, follow M-38 west of Baraga and turn south onto Prickett Dam Road (also called Forest Road 193), marked by a national forest sign. Within 11 miles the road merges into Sturgeon Gorge Road (Forest Road 191), and a few hundred yards to the right there is a sharp 90-degree curve. At this bend an extremely rough jeep trail leads west to the edge of the gorge. It is best to walk the quarter mile that ends at one of the most beautiful panoramas in the U.P. You see the deep gorge below and miles of forested ridges and hills to the west.

A mile before reaching Sturgeon Gorge Road, you will pass another jeep trail leading off to the west. From the jeep trail a foot path winds a mile down the steep bank of the gorge, which can be slippery during wet weather, to the roaring Sturgeon River Falls.

The history and color of the Keweenaw Peninsula can be seen in a variety of unique bars and restaurants throughout the area. Houghton, home of Michigan Tech University and a departure point for Isle Royale National Park, has several. Best known is the recently renovated Douglas House, a saloon since 1860 and listed on the National Register of Historic Places. Less known but just as interesting is the **Library Bar and Restaurant** tucked away among the stone buildings on North Isle Royale Street. The building was constructed in 1890, and for almost its entire history it has housed some kind of saloon and restaurant. In 1967, it was named the Library and has an interesting interior that includes, of course, books but also an in-house newspaper that doubles as a menu. Between the descriptions of sandwiches, prime rib dinners, salad bar, and homemade desserts are tidbits of history and little-known facts about a variety of subjects. The menu makes for interesting reading; the food makes for an excellent meal. The Library (906-482-6211) is open from 11:30 A.M. until 1 A.M. Monday through Saturday and from noon to 5 P.M. Sunday. Prices for sandwiches range from $2 to $5, for complete dinners from $5 to $11.

In nearby Lake Linden, right downtown on Calumet Avenue, is the **Lindell's Chocolate Shop**. Joseph Bosch had the building erected in 1893 for his Bosch Brewing Company, but in 1918 it was refurbished with wooden ceiling fans, twenty high-backed oak booths, a nickelodeon, leaded-glass windows, and a 6-foot-long marble food preparation table that took four people to lift. It became the Chocolate Shop, and though the entire building was moved down the street in 1928, little of the interior has changed since then.

The menu has, however, as the shop no longer makes candy but specializes in homemade ice cream. Richard and Francis Grunow took over the business in 1977 and still use the 1943 ice cream maker that is proudly displayed in the shop's front window. You can arise at 4 A.M. any day and watch Grunow make the ice cream, or you can come by at a more reasonable hour and taste one of the four or five flavors he turns out. Lindell's Chocolate Shop (906-296-0793) is also a restaurant and bar with a full menu, but unquestionably it is the ice cream and the malts, milk shakes, sundaes, and banana splits that are its most popular items. The shop is open from Monday through Thursday from 7 A.M. until 7 P.M. and on Friday and Saturday from 7 A.M. to 9 P.M.; it is closed on Sunday.

Keweenaw County

Under the forceful will of President Andrew Jackson, Michigan became a state in 1837 when it grudgingly accepted the entire U.P. in exchange for surrendering Toledo to Ohio. In only six years, this "worthless wilderness" became the land of incredible wealth after Douglas Houghton, the first state geologist, explored the Keweenaw Peninsula and reported finding chunks of pure copper. Miners began arriving by 1841, and within two years there was a lively copper rush to this small section of the U.P., forcing the U.S. Army to build Fort Wilkins in Copper Harbor (today a state historical park) to maintain law and order. As in all

Calumet Opera House

stampedes for a precious metal, many mines quickly died, and thousands went home disillusioned and broke. But substantial lodes of copper were uncovered, and by the 1860s this area was producing 15 million pounds annually or almost 90 percent of the national total. Two of the most profitable mines were Calumet and Hecla, and near them sprang up the town of Red Jacket. Later renamed Calumet, this city of 66,000 in 1898 had wealth, importance (it was being considered as a new site for the state capital), and a peculiar problem.

Due to large contributions to the city budget from the mines, the council found itself with a surplus of funds. Already the community had paved streets, electric lights, and telephones, so the town decided to build an opera house, the grandest theater in the Midwest, one that would rival the stages on the East Coast. The **Calumet Opera House** was built on the corner of Sixth and Elm streets in 1899, and no expense was spared. It was designed in an Italian Renaissance style and inside featured two balconies, private viewing chambers along the walls, and rococo plaster ornamentation of gilt, cream, and crimson. The acoustics were near perfect: An actor could whisper on the stage and be heard in the last row of the top balcony.

On March 20, 1900, the first performance was given to a packed house of 1,100 and was described by the *Copper Country Evening News* as "the greatest social event ever known in the copperdome's metropolis." A string of legendary performers arrived at the famed opera house, including John Philip Sousa, Sarah Bernhardt, Douglas Fairbanks, and Lillian Russell. Eventually the theater, like the town, fell upon hard times. The local mines, the last to operate in the Keweenaw Peninsula, were closed for good due to a labor strike in 1968; by then Calumet's population had dwindled to 1,000.

The mines are still closed, but the opera house has since reopened. Declared a National Historic Site in 1974, it was fully restored and its opulence can be viewed Monday through Friday from 10 A.M. until 5 P.M. There is no admission for a peek into Calumet's past. It has also returned to live stage after a stint with motion pictures in th 1920s and 1930s; major performances are scheduled from March through October. Call for information (906-337-2610).

Next door to the opera house is **Shute's Bar**, which features what many say is the oldest wooden bar and back bar in the state. Both date to 1893 when Marco Curto, an immigrant miner who saved his pay, opened up Curto's Saloon. One of forty-six saloons in the area, it was a place where immigrant miners could always find someone who spoke their native tongue. The bar is massive and polished to a shine as is the back bar, which includes a huge mirror, wooden coolers, a metal cash register, and two intriguingly carved liquor cabinets that are 10 feet tall. The whole unit is crowned by a spectacular colored glass canopy. The long, narrow saloon also has the original booths and a ceiling and archway featuring classic trim and plaster work. Shute's is not just a place to have 45-cent beer; it's a proper complement to the historic opera house next door.

At one time or another in the late 1800s, there were fourteen active copper mines in the Keweenaw Peninsula, and today a number of them have been preserved, offering a glimpse of the underground world of the miners. The least promoted but perhaps the most intriguing is the **Delaware Mine** on US-41 between Calumet and Copper Harbor. To reach it you pass through Delaware, a ghost town of a half dozen abandoned buildings and a sobering reminder that when the copper ran out, so did the lifeblood for boom towns throughout the peninsula. Interest in the copper at Delaware began in 1845 and involved one early investor by the name of Horace Greeley. The famous newspaper editor actually made a trip to the Keweenaw Peninsula but never traveled much farther than Eagle River. A mining company was organized in 1848, and actual mining began the following year. From 1849 to 1851 the mine produced 522,541 pounds of copper, but the Northwest Copper Mining Company lost almost $100,000 on the operation. The mine was sold again and again to new investors, with one company building a huge hoist house in 1870 to pull the cars out of the deep shafts that were being dug. But the Delaware never really turned a profit, and the shafts were sealed for good in 1887. The town of Delaware, which in 1879 had 300 residents, also disappeared.

Now a tourist attraction, the Delaware is the only mine you can explore on your own. You begin by donning a hardhat and descending a 100-foot staircase through shaft Number 1 into the first level. The top level is 900 feet of tunnel from which other passages, shafts, and a huge cavern can be viewed. Nine other levels extend 1,400 feet below it, but underground streams have long since flooded all but the first. There is still plenty of copper lying around in this level, and in the information center visitors are told how to recognize and search for it in the mine and then given tips afterward on cleaning any metal they find.

You can also explore the remains of the hoist house above ground and get a good overview of the ghost town and nearby rides from the parking lot. The Delaware Mine (906-289-4688) is open from Memorial Day until mid-October from 10 A.M. until 6 P.M. daily. There is an admission fee.

The men who actually worked the mines were often immigrants from the Cornwall area of England or from Finland or Norway, and they brought to Copper Country their strong ethnic heritage. Traces of that heritage can be seen in the Cornish pasties, which are sold throughout the U.P., and in the popularity of Finnish saunas. For years the sauna took the place of bathtubs and showers in homes, as early settlers would build their sauna huts first and worry about their cabins later. A good sauna begins with a shower to open up the pores of the skin, followed by a stay in a cedar-paneled room where a small pile of rocks are heated. As water is tossed on the rocks, a dry heat emerges that makes the body perspire profusely, flushing out dirt and grime from the skin. The temperature ranges from 160 to 180 degrees, and the old miners used wicker sticks to beat their backs and get the blood moving. The entire ordeal is ended with a cold shower to close the pores.

In Copper Harbor, you experience this Finnish ritual at **Brockway Sauna**, operated by Minnetonka Resort in the heart of town on US-41. The public sauna is across the street from the resort and consists of four private suites. Each one is completely paneled in cedar and features a dressing area, shower, and sauna that will seat four to six people. The building is not that far from the shores of Lake Superior, and occasionally a local person will finish the sauna with a mad dash into the chilly lake, a tradition most visitors pass up.

The Brockway Sauna (906-289-4449) is open daily from May 15 to Oct. 15 from 1 P.M. until 10 P.M. The price includes use of a room, towel, soap, and a wicker stick if you request it.

Keweenaw is the smallest county in the U.P., but it has more than its share of scenic drives, where every curve reveals another striking view. The most famous is the Brockway Mountain Drive, a 10-mile stretch to Copper Harbor that is the highest above-sea-level drive between the Rockies and Alleghenies. Less traveled but almost as scenic in its own way is **Sand Dune Drive** between Eagle River and Eagle Harbor. From Eagle River this portion of M-26 heads west along the Lake Superior shoreline, climbing high above the water along sandy bluffs. The road provides sweeping views of the Great Lake on the horizon and the sandy shoreline below, and the best turnoff looms above Great Sand Bay. The road returns to the lake level at Cat Harbor, a delightful beach for sunning and swimming if you can handle Superior's chilly waters, and then swings through Eagle Harbor, passing the picturesque Eagle Harbor Lightstation, which is now a museum open to the public.

From Eagle Harbor M-26 continues east, first passing the junction to Brockway Mountain Drive and then returning to the edge of Lake Superior, whose shoreline becomes a rugged mass of red sandstone, gracefully carved by the pounding waves. Along this segment you will pass Devil's Wash Tub, a huge depression in the shoreline that echoes the waves crashing in and out of it.

Ontonagon County

Three miles west of Silver city is **Porcupine Mountains Wilderness State Park**, a preserve of 58,000 acres of primitive forests, secluded lakes, and the rugged "Porkies." For most visitors, this state park is a quick drive to the end of M-107, where they follow a short wooded path to the Escarpment, which overlooks Lake of Clouds, a watery gem in between the peaks and ridges of the mountains. But those willing to don a pair of hiking boots can enjoy some of the most unusual accommodations found in the U.P. with a night in one of the park's rustic cabins.

Within the Porkies is a trail network of more than 85 miles, and scattered along the footpaths are sixteen wilderness cabins, each located in a scenic setting along a stream, lake, or on the shoreline of Lake Superior. You can only reach them on foot, and some are an all-day hike while others lie only thirty or forty minutes from the nearest parking lot. The cabins have no electricity, running water, or toilets that flush. Modern conveniences are replaced by candles, wood stove, and an outhouse up the hill. But they are ideal for anybody who wants to spend a night in the woods without having to "rough it" in a tent, sleeping on the ground.

Cabins provide bunks, mattresses, cooking utensils, and in the case of those on an inland lake, a small rowboat. You must provide sleeping bag, clothing, and food. The park rents the cabins, which hold from four to eight people, from April through November at $24 per night. Stop at the park visitor's center just off M-107 (open daily from 10 A.M. until 6 P.M.) for maps and a list of open cabins. Call (906-885-5275) or write ahead of time for information and a cabin reservation to Porcupine Mountains Wilderness State Park, 599 M-107, Ontonagon, MI 49953.

Gogebic County

Waterfalls of every type and description are the gems of the Upper Peninsula, and there are more than 150 of them scattered across this region of Michigan. But **Black River Harbor Drive** (also known as Black River Road and County Road 513) in Gogebic County is virtually a parkway of whitewater splendor. The 15-mile road departs from Bessemer on US-2 and enters Ottawa National Forest, ending at scenic Black River Recreation Area on Lake Superior. Heading north you first pass Copper Peak Ski Flying Hill, the largest artificial ski slide in the world and the site of 500-foot jumps during the winter. In the summer visitors take the chairlift and elevator to the top for a view of three states and Canada.

From Copper Peak, Black River Road enters the heart of the national forest and winds near five waterfalls, each lying at the end of a trail from a marked turnoff. Gorge and Potawatomi falls are among the the most spectacular and easiest to reach. The two falls are within 800 feet of each other and only a five-minute walk from the parking lot. Potawatomi is the largest with a 130-foot-wide cascade that drops 30 feet into the Black River. Gorge, smaller with a 24-foot drop, is encased in a steep and narrow red rock canyon—a spectacular setting. A well-marked path with stairs and observation decks leads you past both falls.

At the end of the road you can camp at Black River Harbor Recreation Area or those who desire a little more luxury can rent a log cabin at **Bear Track Inn** nearby. The small resort has been around since the 1930s, when it catered to lumbermen and commerical fishermen. Its name came from a hungry bear who wandered in one night when they were building the main cabin and walked in the wet cement of the front steps. The name stuck and the track can still be seen today. The inn has only three cabins for rent, but two are authentic log structures and all three feature natural wood interior, wood stoves and stone fireplaces, and kitchen facilities. The large cabin can sleep ten, the others hold four people each, and during the summer they rent for $33 per night for double occupancy. Call the inn (906-452-6364) for reservations or write Bear Track Inn, 15325 Black River Road, Ironwood, MI 49938.

Iron County

Perhaps the U.P.'s largest and least-known historical complex is **Iron County Museum**, located in the village of Caspian on County Road 424, 2 miles south of US-2 at Iron River. The grounds include almost twenty buildings, many a century old, in a Greenfield Village–like setting that lacks some of the polish of the famous Dearborn attraction but is no less interesting. The park occupies the site of the Caspian Iron Mine, and the head frame that hoisted cars out of the mine in the 1920s still towers over the complex. The main museum is the former engine house, which has been considerably enlarged and today is a maze of displays and three-dimensional exhibits. The favorite is the iron ore mining model that for a nickel will actually run through the process of the rock being raised from the mine and loaded into railroad cars above ground. Other interesting exhibits are the renovated saloon, blacksmith shop, and schoolroom and a hand-carved model of a logging camp that fills an 80-foot display case with hundreds of figures and pieces.

Outside you can wander through one historic building after another: a logging camp bunkhouse with a table set for supper and mackinaw shirts (made of a heavy plaid wool) still hanging up near the door, a barn filled with plows and threshers of the 1800s, a completely furnished homesteader's cabin, and so on. You could easily spend an entire day exploring this fascinating folk life complex. Iron County Museum (906-265-2617) is open from mid-May to October from 9 A.M. to 5 P.M. Monday through Saturday and 1 to 5 P.M. Sunday. There is a small admission fee.

Dickinson County

As in the copper fields, many workers in iron mines were immigrants from Europe. In Iron Mountain, many Italians came to work the Chapin Mine, which was discovered in 1879, and went on to become the second-leading ore producer in the U.P. You can learn about the miner's life and work at the Menominee Range Historical Museum and see the huge water pump that was built for the exceptionally wet mine at the Cornish Pump and Mining Museum. Or you can enjoy a lively night and a delicious Italian dinner in the old neighborhood.

The Stables, a restaurant on Fourth Avenue off of US-2, is located in the middle of Iron Mountain's eighteen-block Italian neighborhood. The building was constructed in 1897 to serve as a local pub until prohibition changed the business into Pietranto-nio & Sons Fancy Groceries. Once prohibition ended it quickly returned to serving beer; some doubt that it ever stopped. In 1980, Butch Hoyum took over the dilapidated bar, restored its historic decor, and turned it into a fine Italian restaurant while retaining its ethnic quality and the friendliness found in all good neighborhood pubs. He understood what it took because his mother was Italian—"the only reason they accept me around here."

In The Stables, they still refuse to serve meat on Fridays, which is okay with non-Catholic patrons because the fish fry is superb. As expected, there is also excellent homemade Italian cuisine including polenta, gnocchi, and ravioli, or you can enjoy a draft beer at what Hoyum claims is the second-oldest bar in the U.P. (Shute's in Calumet is older.) Dinner is priced from $4 to $8 for pasta; prices are higher for other entrees. The Stables (906-774-0890) is open from 10 A.M. until 10 P.M. Monday through Saturday and 5 to 9 P.M. on Sunday. Dinner reservations are recommended.

The Menominee River forms almost half of the border between Wisconsin and Michigan's Upper Peninsula, beginning west of Iron Mountain and extending to its mouth on Green Bay. Two miles south of Norway the river flows through Piers Gorge, a whitewater area of large falls, holes, and swirls as the river tumbles through a scenic forested canyon. The gorge picked up its name in the 1840s when loggers built piers along this section of the river in an attempt to slow down the current and prevent logs from jamming and splitting on the jagged rocks. You can view this spectacular stretch of wild water by heading south of Norway on US-8; just before its bridge across the Menominee, turn left onto Piers Gorge Road. The paved road quickly turns into a dirt one, and then after 0.6 mile it ends at a footpath. A hike of 0.8 mile brings you to a series of viewing points above the falls.

During the summer you can also experience the gorge and what many rafters call the "Midwest's premier whitewater river" through the **Roaring Rapids Raft Company**. The company offers a three-hour raft trip that takes you through Piers Gorge and over its falls. On Saturday and Sunday, the rafters meet at the US-8 bridge at 9 A.M. and again at 2 P.M. and then proceed to the river with their large inflated rafts. It's a wild ride, one that will leave you soaking wet but exhilarated. The company provides the rafts, guides, helmets, life jackets, and a paddle for each passenger.

Roaring Rapids Raft Company (715-757-3300) is based in Wisconsin and has been running the Piers Gorge operation for fourteen years. The cost for the raft trips, which also can be set up during the week by advance reservation, is $21 per person.

Appendix

The following are state and regional tourist offices, which can provide the most up-to-date information on accommodations, restaurants, and attractions in their area:

Michigan Travel Bureau
P.O. Box 30226
Lansing, MI 48909
Toll-free number: 800-543-2937

East Michigan Tourist Association
One Wenonah Park
Bay City, MI 48706
(517-895-8823)

Southeast Michigan Travel and Tourist Association
64 Park Street
P.O. Box 1590
Troy, MI 48099
(313-585-8220)

West Michigan Tourist Association
136 Fulton Street, East
Grand Rapids, MI 49503
(616-456-8557)

Upper Peninsula Travel and Recreation Association
618 Stephenson Avenue
P.O. Box 400
Iron Mountain, MI 49801
(906-774-5480)

Index

Index

About the Author

Jim DuFresne is a Detroit-based travel and outdoor writer whose syndicated column, "Travels in Michigan," appears in daily newspapers across the state. Formerly a sports and outdoors editor for the *Juneau Empire* in Alaska, DuFresne published his first travel book, *Tramping in New Zealand*, in 1982. His other books include *Isle Royale National Park, Voyageurs National Park, Alaska: A Travel Survival Kit*, and *Glacier Bay National Park: A Backcountry Guide to the Glaciers and Beyond*. The author of six children's books as well, DuFresne is currently working on *A Guide to Michigan State Parks*.

"Off the Beaten Path" series

EDITIONS AVAILABLE

Colorado • Florida • Georgia • Illinois • Indiana
Michigan • Minnesota • New Jersey • New York
Northern California • Ohio • Pennsylvania
Southern California • Virginia • Wisconsin

◆

"Recommended Country Inns" series

EDITIONS AVAILABLE

New England • Mid-Atlantic and Chesapeake Region
The South • The Midwest • West Coast
Rocky Mountain Region • Arizona, New Mexico, and Texas

Don't be puzzled about Michigan.

Learn about your state, and others, with the enjoyable
and educational 100-piece jigsaw puzzles in the
Austin-Peirce 'Puzzlin' State" puzzle series.